YOUR
Y2K
PERSONAL
PROTECTION PLAN

YOUR

Y2K

PERSONAL
PROTECTION PLAN

Jim Hickman

HarperCollins*Publishers*

All statements made herein are year-2000 statements and are protected as year-2000 readiness disclosures under the Good Samaritan Act of 1998.

The information contained in this document represents the personal views of the author, Jim Hickman. It is intended to be the author's interpretation of the year-2000 computer problem (Y2K) at the time of its writing. The extent of possible Y2K computer problems cannot be forecast precisely. Furthermore, the organizations subject to the greatest impact refuse to disclose what they know about their vulnerability. Therefore, the views of the author are subjective and based solely upon his study of public information and conversations with colleagues. Each reader must make an individual judgment about the accuracy and the use of this document.

Information provided in this document is provided "as is," without warranty of any kind, either express or implied, including but not limited to the implied warranties of merchantability, fitness for a particular purpose, and freedom from infringement.

CONTENTS

ACKNOWLEDGMENTS

This book is dedicated to my lovely wife, Caroline, who first envisioned the monthly program and without whom I might not have finished before the year 2000. It is written for our kids, Elliott and Galen, and for children everywhere who will bring the new millennium to fruition.

Sincere gratitude is due to Howard Schiffer and Ken Wright, who provided the inspiration, the opportunity, and the marketing savvy to bring this book to life. My editors at HarperResource, Lois Brown and John Atkins, and the staff at HarperCollins, have performed exceptionally to produce a finished book.

I express my deepest thanks to Marlow Hotchkiss for his assistance in crafting this program to meet your needs. Special thanks go to Trish Palmer, who organized the vast resources on this subject into a manageable presentation. Gigi Coyle deserves recognition for her unending belief in and support for my attempts to make the world a better place.

I especially thank the individuals who inspired me to embrace Y2K: Ganga White, John Steiner, Margot King, Tracy Rich, Michael Tantleff, John Danner, Dennie LaTourelle, Keith Witt, and my mother.

Designing this program would not have been possible without the support of Doug Carmichael, Margaret Wheatley, Tom Atlee, Gordon Davidson, Robert Theobald, Bayard Stockton, Mark Phillips, Steve Davis, John Peterson, Joel Ackerman, Eric Utne, Michael Levett, Kim Cranston, Judy Laddon, Terry Moore, John Davis, Donna Gianoulis, Danielle LaPorte, Roger Macdonald, and Elye Pitt.

The information in this manual is a compilation from multiple sources readily available for further study. I include enough detail to support my approach but not to duplicate those provided by more informed specialists from whom I have liberally borrowed. I gratefully acknowledge and thank the dozens of committed individuals who, like me, have reorganized their lives in order to help others become more prepared for the year 2000.

PREFACE

I offer this information to assist you in educating your family and friends and to help them grapple with the implications of the Y2K problem. By following the program outlined here, you can turn Y2K uncertainty and possible disruption into an opportunity for true security and a deeper experience of community. Good luck on your journey toward preparing yourself, your home, and your family and friends for the year 2000.

INTRODUCTION

Four decades ago, when computers were in their infancy, memory was precious. To conserve storage space, programmers reduced four-digit years to two-digit years—so, for example, *1960* became *60*. The computers were further instructed to assume that all two digit-years would be preceded by the digits *19*. Hence, *60* means *1960*. When the year 2000 *(00)* arrives, many computers around the world will believe it is the year 1900 instead of the year 2000.

Some of these same computers control nearly every system that keeps the world running—telephones, electricity, gasoline production, banking services, household water delivery, business operations, and most government agencies. Misinterpreting *00 as 1900 will cause the computers to stop working. This simple error threatens to collapse the very fabric upon which our global society rests.*

Imagine a gigantic electronic tidal wave that hits the entire country all at once. Those people who saw it coming and have life jackets and a rubber boat will be much better off than those who didn't bother to prepare. This manual will prepare you for the tidal wave should it hit your neighborhood.

Remember that no one knows exactly what will happen. Many authorities believe the problems will be severe and last for several months; others predict only minor difficulties that will be fixed during January. Experts do agree that some disruptions will occur.

It is essential, therefore, that every American family develop some backup systems that can replace short-term breakdowns in the normal supply of goods and services. The question everyone asks is, "For how many days should I be prepared to live without normal services?" There is no single answer for everyone.

I recommend that you and your family be capable of living self-sufficiently for at least two weeks and, if possible, for a month. This approach will protect you from any significant discomfort during the early months of 2000.

Why Do I Recommend a Fourteen-to-Thirty-Day Plan?

- I believe that a minimum of two weeks of disruptions is probable in most of America and that some regions will suffer longer-lasting effects.

- Many families cannot afford to store more than a two-week supply of goods, and it is important that everyone has a minimal reserve for Y2K.

- Current manufacturing capabilities could not respond to the demand if millions of Americans began stockpiling goods for more than four weeks.

- If a thirty-day supply is more than the emergency requires, during the recovery period you will be able to assist others who were less prepared.

Preparing for Y2K disruptions requires that you plan alternatives to your normal sources of basic services, utilities, and goods. If telephone service is not available, how will you communicate outside your home? If the gas and electricity are shut off, how will you keep warm during January? If there are temporary food shortages, will you be able to feed your family? Do you have enough supplies to provide for your normal daily personal needs? Planning for these contingencies will bring you a greater sense of security as we approach the new year.

The following chapters detail how and when to develop your alternatives. You can easily be prepared for thirty days of self-sufficient living by choosing what is appropriate for your situation from the guidelines that are presented. Check off the "Done" box as each task is completed.

The actions that we and our families take throughout 1999 will, in my opinion, determine the outcome of the year 2000. We can panic and, by our actions, contribute to a collapse of the system. Or we can educate ourselves and make appropriate plans to protect our families and our communities.

I think you'll agree it's best to be prepared well in advance. Use this information in whatever way seems most beneficial to you, and be sure to share it with your loved ones and neighbors. If you work together on the "Y2K Monthly Program," chances are you'll be ready for whatever Y2K brings!

Remember, hope for the best, but prepare for the rest!

YOUR Y2K PERSONAL PROTECTION PLAN

Chapter 1

TELEPHONE, TELEVISION, AND RADIO

Telephone service

When you place a long-distance telephone call, your voice is changed into millions of bits of information that travel through thousands of miles of plastic cable or just through the air itself and are transferred across dozens of switches in many locations. This vast network of communication technologies is used daily to send billions of dollars around the world, manage the distribution of electricity throughout the United States, tell trucks and trains where their freight is needed, and keep the global economy alive and running. For you and me this means that we can cash a check with ease, turn on our television for the evening news, buy whatever we need at the corner store, and have some job security throughout our lives.

The telephone networks are run by computer software and embedded chips. Your monthly telephone bills are calculated from computerized call records. These networks and their billing capabilities rely on hundreds of millions of computer instructions that must be ready for the year 2000. It will cost over $2 billion to make sure they can all run flawlessly in the twenty-first century. Though significant progress has been made in recent months, the large number of telephone companies that must be ready presents a significant risk of Y2K failures in this most important of industries.

Television and Radio Stations

Network television programming is mostly produced at a central location and distributed to local affiliates through satellite and land-based telephone circuits. News reports are usually recorded at the sight of a news event and transmitted back to the studio using similar telephone circuits. If the telephone service is not operational because of Y2K problems, this information cannot reach the transmitters that deliver the programs to your home.

Both television and radio stations are now highly computerized. The recording and broadcasting equipment use embedded chips that are sometimes dependent on dates, and most news reports are dated by computers for ease of filing in a station's archives. All of the advertising that keeps commercial television and radio alive is managed by computers. Each of these aspects of the broadcast industry is susceptible to Y2K breakdowns.

On the positive side most large television and radio stations have emergency generators to supply power in case of a local electrical failure, so they will continue to broadcast the news if all other systems are functioning normally. Every community has a designated emergency-broadcast station that is part of the national Emergency Alert System. Identify that station in your community, and be confident that you will have access to information on New Year's Day and beyond.

What Does This Mean for You and Your Family?

- Telephones might not work. Telephone failures may prevent access to emergency medical, police, and fire services.

- 911 emergency lines might not work.

- You might not be able to do your job or to operate a business.

- Electronic banking might stop.

- Your television and radio may not function during January and February 2000, when information about the rest of the world will be essential.

What Can You Do?

Communication will be extremely important if normal services are unreliable.

1. Have access to an alternative means of communication.

   - *Citizens-band (CB) radio:* Uniden and Cobra make excellent products (available at most consumer-electronics stores).

   - *Motorola Talkabout walkie-talkies:* Keep an adequate battery supply (available in most consumer electronics stores).

   - *Ham radio:* Consult the on-line *Beginner's Guide to Ham Radio*: http://www.irony.com/ham-howto.html

   - Cellular telephones might continue to function normally in some locations.

I will need the following resources to communicate with family and friends:

☐

_____

_____

_____

_____

Important phone numbers:

☐

_____

_____

_____

_____

_____

_____

_____

2. Buy a radio or TV that does not depend on mains (AC) electricity.

   - *Emergency Alert System hand-held radio:* Automatic alert during emergencies with information about natural and technological disasters as well as recovery efforts. Available from Oregon Scientific, Inc. (800–869–7779).

   - *Community low-power radio station:* Encourage establishment of a community low-power FM radio station that can operate on 12V batteries (www.radio4all.org).

   - *Shortwave radio (battery operated):* Keep an adequate battery supply. Available at any consumer electronics store or at Kansas Wind Power (785–364–4407).

   - *Hand-crank radio (Freeplay AM/FM):* Some have a solar-power option. Available from Real Goods Renewables (800–919–2400), Y2K Solutions Group (888–925–4968), or Kansas Wind Power (785–364–4407).

   - *Battery-powered television:* Keep an adequate battery supply. Available at most television stores.

☐ Battery-operated televisions and radios, and batteries I require:

_____

_____

_____

_____

_____

☐ My community emergency broadcast station is: _____

3. Make special arrangements with relatives, employers, and business associates before December 31.

4. Join with neighbors to make backup emergency arrangements with local fire and police departments, hospitals, and so on.

Your Y2K Personal Protection Plan

I will need to make personal, business, and neighborhood arrangements in advance as follows:

_____

_____

_____

_____

_____

_____

_____

_____

_____

Reliable communication and information are the key to surviving Y2K. Getting up-to-date news and being able to stay in touch with loved ones will make the difference between anxiety and security.

Chapter 2

ELECTRICITY AND HEAT

Electricity (The Power Grid)

The U.S. electric power system is made up of some 7,800 power generating plants (including nuclear power plants) where electricity is created and 112,000 substations that distribute it to you through local utility companies. To maintain a constant flow of electricity to your home, utility companies use computers and telecommunications to coordinate this distribution among themselves. So if the telephone system fails, electricity will not be delivered to your home for very long.

When you awaken each day, you expect your alarm clock to be accurate, the coffeemaker to brew reliably, and the television to deliver the morning news. You can rely on this routine because thousands of computers in your local utility company are making certain that every household receives an even flow of electricity. At a Honolulu electric company, which recently simulated the year 2000 rollover, computer software failures caused too much electricity to go to some customers and too little to go to others. If you had awakened to those conditions, your clock might have run too fast, your coffeemaker might have overheated, and your television might have burned out. Or all of your appliances might not work for lack of electricity.

Geographically, electricity networks in the US are divided into four separate and relatively independent regions. A Y2K disruption in one part of a regional network could affect that entire region but would not necessarily affect the entire national system. However, because many utility companies use identical equipment in their networks, a Y2K failure in one system would likely fail in all systems, causing widespread electrical outages and, possibly, electrical shortages for several weeks.

Approximately 20 percent of our electricity is generated by nuclear power plants that are seriously at risk from Y2K computer failures, 40 percent comes from coal-burning plants that depend on regular fuel delivery by railroads, and about 30 percent comes from natural gas. Both the railroad and natural gas industries are seriously behind schedule in fixing their computer systems. This interconnectedness has influenced many power-industry experts to admit privately that power outages are likely beginning in January 2000.

Gas and Oil Supplies

Staying warm in the winter could be a problem in January 2000. Deliveries of the oil and natural gas we use to heat our homes, our hot water, and our offices might be interrupted because nearly every aspect of their production and distribution depends on computer technology.

Every offshore oil platform has approximately ten thousand embedded chips. Many of these are below the surface of the ocean and cannot be replaced before the turn of the century. In late 1998 Chevron reported that it will not fix all its systems by December 31, 1999. It also acknowledged that year-2000 business interruptions could prevent it from producing oil and gas and delivering refined products to its markets.

What about gas for your car? Gasoline shortages are a possibility. Those underground tanks at your local gasoline stations might have little or no gas in them early next year. And even if gasoline is available, most stations are dependent on electricity to pump the gasoline, so power failures may prevent access to the fuel.

What Does This Mean for You and Your Family?

- You might be without power for some time.

- Heating oil and natural gas might be scarce or deliveries might be postponed.

- Gasoline shortages might occur. Using your car might become too expensive.

- Stores and businesses might close.

- Emergency services might be unavailable.

What Can You Do?

Investigate the most cost-effective alternatives to local utilities. Some people can afford their own backup systems, but others cannot. Everyone should discuss these alternatives with their neighbors to see where it's possible to share resources.

1. Have adequate contingency plans for power failures.

   - Generator with extra fuel: multifuel generators are available from Sears, Master Distributors (800–446–1446), Mayberry Sales and Service (877–414–6632). Diesel generators are available from China Diesel Imports (619–669–1995), Kubota Tractor Corp. (310–370–3370), RJK Power (888–436–0172).

   - Camping stove and/or barbecue grill with extra fuel: these are available at most camping stores, including Sears, Wal-Mart, L. L. Bean (800–221–4221), Campmor (800–226–7667), Emergency Preparedness Service (888–626–0889), Volcano Corporation (888–532–9800).

   - 120-hour candles are available from the Y2K Solutions Group (888–925–4968), Emergency Essentials (800–999–1863).

   - Oil lamps or Coleman lanterns for alternative lighting with sufficient fuel reserves are available from most camping stores, Wal-Mart, Real Goods Renewables (800–919–2400), Coleman Company (800–835–3278), Aladdin Mail Order (800–456–1233).

   - Flashlights and spare rechargeable batteries are available at Sears, Wal-Mart, or other superstores.

   - Solar-powered battery rechargers are available from Real Goods Renewables (800–919–2400), Jade Mountain (800–442–1972), Y2K Solutions Group (888–925–4968).

Equipment I require for cooking:

_____

_____

_____

_____

_____

_____

My supplies of fuel, briquettes, matches, etc., are:

_____

_____

_____

_____

_____

_____

_____

□   My supplies of candles, flashlights, and other alternative light sources are:

_____

_____

_____

_____

_____

_____

_____

□   My supplies of batteries and battery rechargers are:

_____

_____

_____

_____

2. Find alternative ways to heat your house or apartment.

- Solar panels for heating water and critical electrical needs are available from Real Goods Renewables (800–919–2400), Jade Mountain (800–442–1972), Y2K Solutions Group (888–925–4968), Backwood Solar Electric Systems (208–263–4290).

- Free-standing wood stove with adequate wood supply, available from Lehman's Non-Electric Supply (330–857–5757), Northern

Tool and Equipment (800–533–5545), Vogelzang International Corp. (888–229–6905).

- Propane gas or kerosene heaters with extra fuel are available from Lehman's Non-Electric Supply (330–857–5757), Real Goods Renewables (800–919–2400), Master Distributors (800–446–1446).

- Heat-reflecting insert for existing fireplace, available from local fireplace vendor, Lehman's Non-Electric Supply (330–857–5757), Y2K Solutions Group (888–925–4968).

- Fire extinguishers are available from Wal-Mart or other superstore.

- Battery-operated smoke/carbon monoxide alarm, available from Wal-Mart or other superstores.

- Warm clothing and sleeping bags.

My alternatives for keeping my home warm are:

_____

_____

_____

_____

_____

_____

_____

_____

2000

☐ I will need wood, fuel, and waterproof matches as follows:

_____

_____

_____

_____

_____

_____

_____

☐ Fire extinguishers and smoke alarms I need:

_____

_____

_____

_____

_____

_____

_____

Warm clothing and bed coverings my family will require:

_____

_____

_____

_____

_____

_____

_____

_____

3. Arrange alternative means of transportation.

   • Get bicycles for the family. Buy saddlebags for supplies and bike carts for young children.

   • Start walking regularly to build up endurance.

   • Organize neighborhood carpools for errands and supplies. Use the most gas-efficient car.

   • Develop alternative means of transportation to work.

Places my family and I will need to travel to:

_____

_____

2000

_____

_____

_____

_____

☐ My transportation alternatives are:

_____

_____

_____

_____

_____

☐ Fuel, repair kits, etc., I will need for alternative transportation:

_____

_____

_____

2000

_____

_____

_____

_____

Names, addresses, and phone numbers for carpool: ☐

_____

_____

_____

_____

_____

_____

_____

_____

_____   ☐

_____

_____

_____

4. Stock up on essentials.

5. Work with neighbors to develop a local contingency plan.

Our neighborhood contingency plans include:

_____

_____

_____

_____

_____

_____

_____

_____

A hundred years ago people lived quite comfortably and safely even though they didn't have the luxuries and appliances we have today. While fuel and power shortages might be inconvenient, if you are prepared, living more simply and relying on family members and neighbors could actually be fun and rewarding. Going forward into the past could be an adventure to remember.

Chapter 3

BANKING, FINANCIAL AFFAIRS, AND INSURANCE

The Banking System

The national banking system is a computer-managed enterprise. Locally, all of the following are vulnerable to a Y2K glitch: ATM transactions; interest calculations; computerized banking records; electronic transfer of funds; and the tracking of loan, deposit, and lease payments. Nationally, banking, investment, or stock market transactions could be affected.

The banking industry is very closely regulated by federal authorities and has been working hard on this problem for up to ten years. The earliest Y2K failures appeared within this industry. Therefore, most banks will almost certainly be prepared to accurately process year 2000 dates.

Banks are highly dependent on electricity and telephone service. Even if bank computers are adjusted for Y2K, without power and telephones ATMs won't work, checks will not clear, and bank records won't be accessible. This will not affect your bank records but might delay your immediate access to your cash deposits.

More important, banks cannot control their customers' level of confidence in their reliability. Therefore, fear of Y2K disruptions, whether real or imagined, might cause you and other customers to withdraw your cash from the bank. Since the amount of cash in bank vaults is not sufficient to meet the needs of all customers, a cautious approach to the accumulation of this cash is advisable. The fear of bank failures must be avoided. Maintain your confidence in our financial institutions.

To guard against the short-term failure of the electrical and telephone systems, including possible bookkeeping problems related to Y2K, I believe that every family should have enough cash to pay for essential expenses through January 2000. This money should be saved from each month's paycheck or gradually withdrawn monthly from your savings or securities accounts through the rest of this year. If we as customers respond thoughtfully to Y2K, banks will continue to operate efficiently into the year 2000. Remember, a run on the banks would hurt all of us and is avoidable through regular savings or withdrawals as described in the "Y2K Monthly Program."

Your Personal Finances

Disruptions or errors that could occur in the computerized files at your bank, the utility or phone companies, your credit card companies, or other similar service providers might cause inaccuracies in your personal financial records. These problems could include: delays in clearing checks, billing errors, inaccurate crediting or debiting of transactions, improper delinquency notices, unwarranted late-payment penalties, or inaccurate credit reporting. You must protect your personal finances by taking appropriate action.

What Does This Mean for You and Your Family?

- Your money will probably be safe but might be unavailable for a short time.

- Banks might close for a while or even fail.

- Automatic payments and deposits might be disrupted.

- Your investments might lose value.

- The economy might suffer significantly.

What Can You Do?

1. Save cash for one month's expenses.

    - In the months leading up to January 2000, accumulate enough cash to pay your essential bills during the month of January in case your source of income is delayed or there is an electrical failure.

- Determine your cash needs and divide by the number of months remaining in this year. This will spread out your savings program to help you achieve your goal and to minimize the impact of last-minute withdrawals on the cash reserves in local banks.

- Refrain from using credit cards in December and January to avoid electronic billing over the date-change period; pay cash for as many bills as possible.

My cash needs for one month:

_____

_____

_____

_____

_____

_____

_____

_____

_____

_____

☐ My plan for saving one-month's cash needs:

_____

_____

_____

_____

_____

☐ Bills that will not be paid by credit card:

_____

_____

_____

_____

_____

_____

_____

2000

2. Limit credit card use to prevent Y2K computer scrambling of your accounts

   - Limit use during December and January. Buy your Christmas presents early this year and have them paid for before December.

   - Save your receipts for all payments and credit card charges.

   - Compare them against your billing statements. Pay special attention to any charges made between December 27 and January 7. Report discrepancies to your card issuer.

Christmas presents to buy before December:

_____

_____

_____

_____

_____

_____

Receipts are stored:

_____

_____

_____

_____

Done

2000

_____

_____

_____

_____

3. Minimize or eliminate debt.

   Remember that even if computer records are lost, eventually your debt will be located with paper records, and the interest will have accumulated.

   • Start a debt-reduction program today.

   • Pay off all credit cards if possible.

   • Consolidate your debts at one institution, i.e., with a home equity loan or credit card with low-interest rates.

☐ Debts I will pay off before January:

_____

_____

_____

_____

_____

_____

_____

Credit cards I will pay off before January and then put away:

_____

_____

_____

_____

_____

_____

2000

Debts that could be consolidated:

_____

_____

_____

_____

_____

_____

_____

2
0
0
0

4. Investigate the readiness of your employer.

- Ask about your employer's Y2K plans and progress.

- Discuss alternative means of transportation to work with your employer and other employees.

- Record systems you use daily in your work, and help your employer determine if they are at risk for Y2K problems.

- Encourage an employee-awareness campaign that informs employees about the company's Y2K preparations and encourages individual preparations.

☐ My employer's Y2K status:

_____

_____

_____

_____

_____

☐ Alternative means to get to work:

_____

_____

_____

_____

_____

Systems at work that could be at Y2K risk:

☐

_____

_____

_____

_____

_____

_____

_____

Y2K preparations to be made at work:

☐

_____

_____

_____

_____

_____

_____

_____

2
0
0
0

5. Reconsider your investment strategy.

- Discuss your investments with your investment counselor.

- Decide what kind of strategy you wish to pursue with Y2K in mind.

- Ask your brokerage house about their Y2K readiness.

  - What are their plans to deal with Y2K?

  - What type of backup records do they keep for such emergencies?

  - What are their contingency plans for identifying and correcting errors in your accounts if Y2K scrambles your information?

- Make certain you have a complete file of all your account statements for 1999.

  - Make a list of all account numbers with current balances.

  - Store records in a safe place.

☐ Financial institutions to contact regarding Y2K:

_____

_____

_____

_____

_____

_____

_____

My Y2K investment strategy:

_____

_____

_____

_____

_____

_____

_____

2000

My file of account statements should include:

_____

_____

_____

_____

_____

_____

_____

☐ My list of account numbers and current balances:

_____

_____

_____

_____

_____

_____

_____

2
0
0
0

6. Organize your essential financial records.

Begin immediately to collect all essential records. This is an easily postponed task. Be sure that you have all your records early in case many people request such documents at the end of the year. When you receive these documents, store them in a safe place, protected against fire, flood, and theft.

- Keep hard-copy records of significant transactions (such as mortgages, stocks, and insurance) during the last quarter of 1999 and January and February 2000.

- Make sure the deposit receipts and periodic statements from your bank and investment company are accurate. Report discrepancies to your financial services provider(s).

- Keep hard copies of bank statements and canceled checks (as proof of payment) for the last quarter of 1999 and January and February 2000. If you bank by computer, download your transaction records before December 31 and store them on a backup disk. Print out your downloaded records in case of computer problems.

- Obtain statements from your creditors detailing your payments toward principal, interest, and other charges. Get a payment schedule showing how your loan balance will decrease until it is paid off.

- If you are able, send payments for mortgages, loans, leases, and other important obligations by certified mail (return receipt requested) for December 1999 and January and February 2000. This will prove that payments were received on time. Canceled checks will suffice for the earlier months in 1999.

- Make certain that you have paper copies of your credit history so you can prove your credit worthiness if records are lost. Obtain copies of your credit report from each of the three major credit bureaus: Equifax (800–997–2493), Experian (800–422–4879), and TransUnion (800–888–4213). Write for these reports during September 1999 and again in January 2000. Check for errors and report them to the credit bureau. Each report will cost about $8.00.

I have hard copies of the following financial records:

_____

_____

_____

_____

_____

_____

_____

☐   I will need hard copies of these financial records:

_____

_____

_____

_____

_____

_____

_____

2
0
0
0

☐   I need statements from the following creditors:

_____

_____

_____

_____

_____

_____

_____

I will make these payments before the year 2000:

_____

_____

_____

_____

_____

_____

_____

_____

I have requested my credit history from:

_____

_____

_____

_____

_____

2
0
0
0

7. Personal records.

The personal records that follow you throughout your life are kept on computers in a variety of agencies. To protect against the loss of such information, you must obtain hard copies (paper copies) of your important personal records. Any records kept by government agencies can be located by VitalChek (800–255–2414). If you don't already have them, send letters formally requesting copies of the following documents:

- birth certificate (city clerk in place of birth)

- Social Security card and Personal Earnings and Benefit Estimate Statement (Social Security Administration office, 800–772–1213)

- marriage and/or divorce records (city clerk in place of marriage or divorce)

- property deeds and other real estate records (city clerk's office), titles, insurance, pensions, and other proofs of all assets owned

- mortgages, credit card and all other loan agreements, court judgments

- property tax records (city clerk's office), income tax returns (800–829–1040), IRS Agreements, W-2 and 1099 earning statements, voter registration records

- educational transcripts and diplomas

☐ I have hard copies of these personal records:

_____

_____

_____

_____

I will need hard copies of the following personal records:

☐

_____

_____

_____

_____

_____

Insurance and Legal

Many organizations and people will seek restitution for Y2K difficulties by turning to lawyers. Analysts estimate there could be $1 trillion in Y2K-related lawsuits. Threat of suits against several software companies have already forced them to offer free Y2K upgrade products; other cases are being prepared that will be very costly. You might have a small business that suffers from Y2K-related problems, find yourself in need of defense against litigation, or need to determine your rights as a consumer. Access to affordable legal advice will be essential.

What Can You Do?

- Check your insurance coverage for Y2K exclusions. Not all insurers are the same. Some domestic insurance coverage has exclusion clauses, but some insurers have not yet excluded such risks. If a power outage disrupts your home's heating system and causes water pipes to freeze and break, will the insurer cover the repair costs? Call your insurance company to understand what risks you face.

- I recommend a legal services policy that I myself carry; it is provided by a company called Pre-Paid Legal Services (PPL). This public company has been in business for twenty-five years and is listed on the American Stock Exchange. For a small monthly fee, PPL provides a family legal plan that provides coverage for a broad range of preven-

2
0
0
0

tive and litigation-related legal expenses. A separate plan for small-business owners provides business-oriented legal service benefits. In Europe, 80 percent of consumers carry this kind of legal services policy. In America, where so many types of insurance are widely accepted, Pre-Paid Legal Services is pioneering a rapidly growing industry. For more information, call 800–431–8974.

Check your insurance policies and determine whether you need a legal insurance policy for Y2K difficulties.

☐ I have read my insurance policy regarding Y2K.

☐ My plan for legal and insurance protection:

_____

_____

_____

_____

_____

For most of us, having enough money is a key to feeling secure. Now, more than ever, it is time to start or increase that savings account. Here is where monthly planning pays off. Setting aside a little bit each month will mean you will have cash in your pocket in the new millennium.

Chapter 4

SYSTEMS INSIDE YOUR HOME

You and Your Home

Your home, and every home in America, is part of the vast network of goods and services that makes up our society. Outside the home we receive goods and services from numerous suppliers who are susceptible to Y2K failures. These include telephone and utilities companies; financial institutions and insurance agencies; health-care and emergency-service providers; and a food-supply chain involving farms, trucks and trains, processing plants, and supermarkets. Inside the home we rely on a variety of Y2K-vulnerable home products such as electronic thermostats, security systems, microwave ovens, VCRs, computers, and fax machines.

As you prepare for Y2K, your first priority is to protect your home and family. This chapter helps you indentify which home products are likely to fail because of Y2K and how to fix them. The rest of the manual describes contingency plans to replace external suppliers whose services to your home might be disrupted because of Y2K. By following the "Y2K Monthly Program," you will be able to fix the systems inside your home and affordably develop backup systems for external failures.

Apartment Buildings

If you live in an apartment, you are likely dependent on many automated systems that manage the building services provided to you and your neighbors. These include security systems, elevators, sprinkler systems, floor lighting, boilers, and trash-disposal systems. Legally, the building owner is responsible for keeping these systems operating. Y2K risks, however, are most effectively eliminated when everyone participates in finding solutions. I recommend that you follow these guidelines:

☐ • Ask the owner or management company about your building's Y2K status.

☐ • Discuss Y2K with your neighbors, and identify actions to be taken collectively.

☐ • Form a committee of unit owners or renters who are willing to work with other residents and building management to set up contingency plans that will meet Y2K emergency needs.

☐ • Pay attention to possible failures of hall lighting, thermostats, garbage-disposal systems, elevators, and security.

Fixing the Systems Inside Your Home
This a three-step process:

1. Identify the most critical systems that must keep working to provide you and your family with basic survival necessities.

2. Identify the daily tools that you depend on each day to keep your life working efficiently and that you would like to have during Y2K disruptions.

3. Determine how to fix them if they have a Y2K problem, or design a backup system if they can't be fixed.

Three forms are enclosed to assist you in this analysis: "Most Critical Systems" and "Daily Tools" assessment forms, and "The List of Y2K At-Risk Home Products." Completed examples of the "Most Critical Systems" and "Daily Tools" forms are included. Using these as a model, fill out the blank forms by listing your own home products. "The List of Y2K At-Risk Home Products" will help you identify which products to include. By completing these checklists, you will be ready to make the necessary corrections or create backup systems in the coming months.

☐ ### Step 1
1. Review the sample "Most Critical Systems" form on page 38. Which of the listed items do you have in your home?

2. Write these items on the "My Home's Most Critical Systems" form on page 39. Add your own items to the list.

3. Fill in the form. The "source of power" indicates if the device will fail because of power outages. The manufacturer is your source of information on whether or not the product will work after the year 2000. "Contact info" tells you where to find out about the product. "Contingency plan" is your backup strategy if the product fails.

Step 2

1. Review the sample "Daily Tools" form on page 40. Which of the listed items do you have in your home?

2. Write these items on the "My Home's Daily Tools" form on pages 41–42. Add your own items to the list.

3. Fill in the form.

Step 3

1. For the products that are most important to you, call the manufacturer and find out whether the product will work after the year 2000.

2. If the answer is "No" or if you cannot get an answer from the company, develop a contingency plan for that item and write it in the appropriate column. For example, how would you keep yourself warm if the furnace didn't work? What would you do with the food in the refrigerator if the electricity failed? How would you get to work or school if your car doesn't start? How would you find out about what is happening elsewhere if the television doesn't work? Review the sample forms for suggestions.

Your home is your castle. It will also be your retreat center for the first weeks of Y2K. By making your home safe and comfortable, even if there are disruptions, you will be doing more for your family's sense of security than almost anything else. Remember Dorothy's motto: "There's no place like home."

MOST CRITICAL SYSTEMS (SAMPLE)

PRODUCT	SOURCE OF POWER	MANUFACTURER MODEL NUMBER	CONTACT INFO	CONTINGENCY PLAN
Furnace	Gas/Electrical*	Lennox	Heating contractor	Fireplace and cordwood, warm clothes, heavy blankets
Thermostat	Battery*	Honeywell	Heating contractor	Fireplace and cordwood, warm clothes, heavy blankets
Telephone	Electrical*	Uniden	800–207–1023	Two old phones that do not require elec.; cell phone
Hot-water Heater	Gas/Pilot light	Nuus	Plumber	Solar water heater
Security system	Electrical*	S.A.S	Bob, phone: 223–8855	Nonelectrical safety locks for windows and doors
Refrigerator	Electrical*	Whirlpool	800–253–1301	Keep freezer closed, open frig. infrequently, eat fresh foods, then frozen, use cooler outdoors for milk, etc.
Clock and alarm	two watches w/ batteries 4 electric clocks			Use travel clocks with batteries

* Electrical is used where product requires electricity provided by local electric company. Battery is used when product has a self-contained source of power.

MY HOME'S MOST CRITICAL SYSTEMS

PRODUCT	SOURCE OF POWER	MANUFACTURER MODEL NUMBER	CONTACT INFO	CONTINGENCY PLAN

2000

DAILY TOOLS (SAMPLE)

PRODUCT	SOURCE OF POWER	MANUFACTURER MODEL NUMBER	CONTACT INFO	CONTINGENCY PLAN
Stovetop	Gas/elec. ignition	Dacor	213–682–2803	Can light with match or use propane camp stove, BBQ
Oven	Electrical	Dacor	213–682–2803	Barbecue and grill in fireplace
Radio AM/FM	Electrical	Sony	800–222–7669	Solar radio w/hand crank for power
Automobile	Petroleum	Toyota	John at Toyota dealer	Bicycles, dog pack, skateboard
Automated water system	Electrical	Rain Bird	800–247–3782	Manually turn on sprinklers, water w/hose
Washing machine	Electrical/Water	Maytag	687–5818	Hand wash
Clothes drier	Gas/Electrical	Maytag	687–5818	Line dry
Fax machine	Electrical/Phone	Brother 1950MC	800–284–4357	
Computer	Electrical/Phone	Power Macintosh 8500	800–767–2775	Catch up on reading, projects, and telephoning
Printer	Electrical	HP LaserJet 5MP	800–752–0900	

MY HOME'S DAILY TOOLS

PRODUCT	SOURCE OF POWER	MANUFACTURER MODEL NUMBER	CONTACT INFO	CONTINGENCY PLAN

2000

MY HOME'S DAILY TOOLS

PRODUCT	SOURCE OF POWER	MANUFACTURER MODEL NUMBER	CONTACT INFO	CONTINGENCY PLAN

2000

Your Y2K Personal Protection Plan

List of Possible Y2K At-Risk Home Products

This list will assist you in identifying those appliances, tools, and items of home equipment that might give you problems around Y2K. (Notes appear at the end of this section on pages 45–46.)

Consumer Electronics

- calculators
- camcorders[1]
- cameras
- clocks and clock radios
- electronic organizers
- home-security systems
- mobile telephones
- monitored security systems[2]
- stationary telephones
- stereo components
- televisions
- VCRs[3]
- voice-message machines

Home Appliances

- air-conditioning systems
- boilers[4]
- clothes driers
- dishwashers
- electric ranges
- freezers

- furnaces[4]

- gas ranges

- heating systems

- microwave ovens

- refrigerators

- thermostats and other temperature-control devices[4]

- washing machines

- water heaters[4]

Home-Office Equipment

- copy machines[5]

- fax machine[6]

- personal-computer hardware

- personal-computer peripherals

- personal-computer software

- printers[5]

- scanners[5]

Other

- automated fire sprinklers

- automated watering systems

- automobiles[7]

- elevators in apartment buildings

- farm and landscape equipment

- generators

- home medical devices

- photographic equipment

- spa and swimming-pool equipment

- wristwatches

Notes on Y2K and Home Products

1. Home products containing microchips might have Y2K problems if they use a month/date/year calendar function. While it is not always possible to determine if this calendar function is in use, most experts agree that, based on this guideline, very few consumer products will have year 2000 problems. To be certain about the Y2K compatibility of a specific product, call the manufacturer's 800 number. Manufacturers have supplied information on the following products:

[1] Camcorder models sold before 1988 will display the date incorrectly after the year 2000 but otherwise will function properly.

[2] Monitored security systems with a calendar function might work fine in your home, but since the information is fowarded to a monitoring company, you must determine if that company's internal systems are compliant. Make such a determination before you contract for service with the company.

[3] In some VCRs the recording of future programs might fail. Those manufactured after 1988 might allow you to manually reset the year to 2000. Pre–1988 models probably will not. Recording and playback functions will not be affected by Y2K.

[4] Furnaces, boilers, water heaters, and related products will not fail or shut down because of Y2K problems. However, if your furnace is controlled by an electronic thermostat or electronic ignition system, your furnace might fail to operate if there are electrical outages.

[5] Scanners, copiers, and printers don't have calendar functions and should not have Y2K problems.

[6] Fax machines have calendar functions, and most recent models will continue to function after the year 2000, according to manufacturers. Some older models will still function but might stamp incorrect dates on incoming and outgoing faxes.

[7] Automobiles use microprocessors in a variety of capacities, including fuel mix in the engine, antilock brakes, airbags, and dashboard displays. According to General Motors, Chrysler, Ford, and Toyota, the few systems that depend on dates have been found to be Y2K-compliant. All of these automobile makers have well-developed Y2K remediation programs and have pledged to notify their customers of any concerns that might arise. For safety I recommend that you do not drive on New Year's Eve and that you exercise caution when you drive for the first time in the new century.

2. If there are electrical failures because of Y2K, resulting power surges could harm electrical products. I recommend protecting your home products with surge protectors—electrical extension cords that contain tiny fuses to insulate your equipment from such electrical fluctuations. They can be obtained at any consumer-electronics store or through your favorite catalog. Be certain that they are in use by December 25.

Fixing Your Personal Computer (PC)

The following section is dedicated to Y2K issues that affect personal computers at home. This information is technical in nature and may not be of interest to those who do not own computers. If this is the case, please simply skip ahead to chapter 5.

If you own an IBM or PC-type personal computer, you must prepare it for the year 2000 rollover. There are several aspects of personal computer use in the home that could be affected: hardware, operating systems, software, and components. Please note that even brand-new computers might not be ready for the year 2000. You cannot be certain without testing.

NOTE: Apple and Macintosh computer hardware and operating systems are not affected by the Year 2000 date problem. Therefore, the sections titled "Upgrading Computer Hardware" and "Upgrading Computer Operating Systems" do not apply to this line of computers. However, please note that software and components on your Apple or Macintosh computer still need to be tested for Y2K compliance.

The following sections present an overview of how your PC may be affected. Check off the "done" box as you complete each of the tasks below.

Upgrade Your Computer's Hardware

All PCs contain a built-in chip that tracks the hour, day, and year. This calendar function, maintained by the real-time clock in the chip, is the master timekeeper for all computer activities. Every PC also contains a second chip (called a BIOS chip) that communicates the time to any software program that uses dates and times. Whenever you turn off your computer, the real-time clock continues to keep track of the time—like a battery-powered clock or watch. When you turn your computer back on, the BIOS chip asks the real-time clock, "What time is it?" The real-time clock electronically signals the exact date and time.

It is similar to calling information for the time. You wake up in the morning and want to know the exact time so you can program your day. You dial a local telephone number, and a computer activates a recorded voice that says, "At the tone, the time will be 5:59 A.M. and twenty seconds." In your PC the message also includes today's date (day, month, year) and the day of the week. The communication of a two- or four-digit year establishes the base time for all computer calculations.

As soon as possible, make sure your computer's chips function with a four-digit year. There are several reliable products available from your local computer store that will diagnose and, in some cases, fix your computer. I recommend the product called Quick Fix 2000 available now from Master Strategies 800–806–4383. Included are two diskettes and easy-to-follow instructions with which you can diagnose and correct the date function in your PC, diagnose all of your software, and receive a printout that describes your computer's Y2K readiness. Many manufacturers offer free Y2K system upgrades for your PC. There are also products available on the Internet. If your PC is more than three years old, you might have to buy and install new internal hardware. Consult a competent computer technician to help you select and install appropriate hardware.

Upgrade Your Computer's Operating Systems

Most recently issued operating systems should be able to handle the year-2000 date change. For example, when Microsoft Windows 98 sees "00" from the BIOS chip, it assumes that the year is actually 2000. Some manufacturers might require you to install a software upgrade. Most companies provide information about the Y2K readiness of their operating systems and any software upgrades through their Web sites and toll-free telephone numbers. Regardless of manufacturer assurances, it is essential that you test your PC operating system before using it in the year 2000.

Upgrade Your Computer's Software

Many off-the-shelf software programs process, store, or display dates. Dates may be used for date stamping and record keeping; retrieving or sorting files and records; making calculations, comparisons, projections and forecasts; or triggering specific actions. Date-sensitive software includes operating systems (see above), databases and spreadsheets (e.g., Excel); accounting, financial, and tax software (e.g., Quicken); contact or project manager programs (e.g., Now-Up-To-Date); utilities, such as file managers and personal information managers; antivirus software (e.g., McAfee or Norton); and fax, E-mail or other communication programs.

Until recently, computer software programs used only two digits to represent the year. Manufacturers are now issuing new programs to replace the ones that will no longer work in year 2000. Any date-sensitive programs you use must be upgraded before January 1, 2000. Contact the manufacturer to obtain new Y2K upgrades (usually free) for these programs, or check with the program's publisher or with software retailers to determine whether any date conversion software is available.

Upgrade Your Computer's Components

Components such as monitors, modems, sound cards, display or graphics cards, TV-tuner cards, and peripheral equipment (like backup drives) also might contain embedded chips. These items might not use a calendar function, but you may want to contact the manufacturer to be sure. For components included in the purchase of your system, contact your computer manufacturer; for components purchased separately, contact the manufacturer of the item.

WARNING: Before you test and correct any year-2000 problems on your personal computer, be sure to back up all of your existing data! Make copies of all your programs, files, and system folders and store them on disks, on a different computer, or on another unconnected storage system.

Consumer Electronics Manufacturers Resource List

Appliances, Electronics

Customer-Service Telephone Numbers

Aiwa	800–424–2499
Altima	800–356–9990
Amana	800–843–0304
Apple	800–767–2775
AST	800–759–4278
ATT	800–222–3111
Audio Source	800–227–5087
Audiovox	800–645–4994
Bel-Tronics	800–828–8804
Blauplunkt	800–323–1943
Bose	800–367–4008
Brother	800–284–4357
Caloric	800–843–0304
Canon	800–828–4040
Casio	800–634–1895
Clarion	800–366–4567
Compaq	800–925–9723; 800–344–4825
Dacor	800–793–0093
Epson	800–922–8911
Eureka	800–822–8064
Fisher	800–421–5013
Frigidaire	800–451–7007
GE	800–447–1700
GE/Hotpoint	800–626–2000
Goldstar	800–541–6808
Harman Int'l	800–645–7484

Harmon Kardon	800–645–7484
Hewlett Packard	800–752–0900
Hitachi	800–369–0422
Hoover	800–940–9200
Honeywell	800–500–9403
IBM	800–772–2227
Infinity	800–645–7484
JBL	800–645–7484
Jensen	800–323–0221
JVC	800–537–5722
Kelvinator	800–323–7773
Kenwood	800–536–9663
Kitchen-Aid	800–253–1301
Koss	800–473–1970
Magic Chef	800–688–1120
Magnavox	877–682–8300
Maytag	800–688–9900
Mitsubishi	800–527–8888
Motorola	800–331–6456
NEC	800–388–8888
Nintendo	800–255–3700
Olympus	800–645–8130
Onkyo	201–825–7950
Packard Bell	800–733–4411
Panasonic	800–638–8876
Philips	800–326–6586
Phonemate	800–247–7889
Pioneer	800–421–1404
Prodigy	800–284–5933
Pyle Industry	800–852–9688
Quasar	201–348–9090

RCA	800–336–1900
Royal	800–321–1134
Samsung	800–524–1041
Sansui	800–421–1500
Sanyo	800–421–5013
Seiko	800–274–4277
Sharp	800–526–0264
Sherwood	800–962–3203
Smith-Corona	800–448–1018
Sony	800–222–7669
Tappan	800–631–3811
Technics	800–638–8876
Texas Instruments	800–842–2737
Toshiba	800–631–3811
Whirlpool	800–253–1301
White-Westinghouse	800–245–0600
Xerox	800–832–6979
Yamaha	800–492–6242
Zenith	877–258–3165

2000

Computers

Year-2000 Sites for Computer Hardware

Apple	www.apple.com/macos/info/2000.html
Compaq	www.compaq.com/year2000
IBM	www.ibm.com/IBM/year2000

Year-2000 Sites for Computer Software

Lotus	www.lotus.com/home.nsf/tabs/Y2K
Microsoft	www.microsoft.com/technet/year2k/product
Norton	www.symantec.com/y2k/y2k.html
Quicken	www.intuit.com/support/year2000.html

Year-2000 Compliance Software for PC

PC Magazine and Ziff-Davis Year 2000 Resource Center	www.8.zdnet.com/pcmag/special/y2k/index.html
QuickFix 2000	877–806–4383
Test 2000	www.righttime.com

Consumer Products

Consumer Electronics Manufacturers Association (CEMA)

www.cemacity.org/cemacity/govt/cema2000.htm

This is a good site from which to obtain numbers and sites for suppliers.

Federal Trade Commission

www.ftc.gov (202–382–4357)

Information Technology Association of America (ITAA)

www.itaa.org/year2000.htm

This is a nonprofit professional computer society tracking Y2K. The site includes links to vendors that provide Y2K products and services.

Vendors

www.vendor2000.com

This is a searchable database of vendors and their products. Usually a link to manufacturer web site is included.

Chapter 5

WATER AND WASTE TREATMENT

Water Supplies and Water-Treatment Systems

In most cities and in many smaller communities, the water purification, distribution, and sanitation systems are susceptible to Y2K interruptions. Water-delivery and waste-disposal facilities contain millions of computer instructions and depend on embedded chips to function properly. These computers manage the purification and flow of your drinking water, the chemical treatment and disposal of your wastewater, and the metering and billing of your water usage. The industry did not, until recently, begin to examine the extent to which this technology is sensitive to the Y2K glitch. In addition, most of these functions depend upon electricity. While most facilities have backup electrical generators, they have a limited supply of fuel.

In Y2K simulations at several facilities, computer malfunctions would have dumped deadly quantities of chemicals into a town's water supply or allowed raw, untreated sewage to be discharged into the surrounding area. These and other potentially enormous health hazards lie in wait for people who live near a treatment plant that is not adequately prepared for the year 2000.

What Does This Mean for You and Your Family?

- Municipal water might be unavailable for an indefinite period.

- Purity or quality of tap water could drop.

- Toilets, showers, and washing machines could be useless.

- Garbage collection might be disrupted.

- Fire hydrants might not work. Safety might be jeopardized.

What Can You Do?

1. Store at least one gallon of water per person per day (two quarts for drinking and two quarts for food preparation and sanitation). If storage space allows, keep two gallons per person per day.

   - *Daily use:* A normally active person needs to drink at least two quarts of water each day, and more is better during emergencies. Children, nursing mothers, and ill people require more. With washing and bathing, most of us use significantly more than one gallon in a normal day. One gallon per person per day requires a substantial reduction in your normal water usage.

   - *Storage:* Good storage containers have three characteristics: they are opaque because light stimulates the growth of bacteria; they are sturdy and not easily broken because of accidents or freezing; and they are stackable to preserve storage space. The least expensive water storage is thoroughly washed recycled plastic containers like milk jugs or soft-drink bottles. Avoid using containers that will decompose or break, such as milk cartons or glass bottles. Never use a container that has held toxic substances. If you wish to purchase containers, I recommend the five-gallon blue plastic water containers available from Walton Feed. Remember that water expands when it freezes, so leave about 15 percent of the volume available for expansion in case the containers freeze.

   - *Sources of drinking water:* In most cases, you will purchase water at your grocery store, from a commercial water supply company, or draw it from your own tap. If you have your own well, make certain it has a hand pump or alternative source of power as backup to electricity.

☐   I plan to store _____ gallons of water for my family.

I will store water in the following types of containers: ☐

_____

_____

_____

_____

_____

_____

_____

My alternative sources of water are: ☐

_____

_____

_____

_____

_____

_____

_____

2. Consider getting water purifiers or portable filter systems for your home.

- *Treatment:* Water that is bacteria-free when stored in clean containers will remain safe throughout this program. Seal the water containers tightly, label the contents and the date, and store them in a cool, dark place.

  If you need to drink water from an uncertain source, you can use water-purification tablets (available at camping stores), Traveler's Friend, the natural treatment for drinking water by NutriBiotic, or boil the water at a rolling boil for at least ten minutes. However, it takes a lot of fuel to boil water, so be attentive to your fuel stores. Keep in mind that some water will evaporate during boiling. Let the water cool before drinking. You can replenish the oxygen content and improve the taste by pouring it back and forth between two containers.

  There are a variety of water filters—either carbon or ceramic—that render water potable. Carbon filters have a high per-gallon cost. I recommend ceramic filters as the better choice. The Katadyn hand-pumped water filter (available at camping supply stores) is the most popular. My family uses one on camping trips and, with some effort, always pumps enough water for our daily needs.

☐ My methods of water purification:

_____

_____

_____

☐ My alternative fuel supply for boiling water is:

_____

_____

_____

3. Explore ways to reuse, recycle, and reserve your water. Develop alternatives for waste disposal.

- *Fill up your bathtub* on December 31 as alternative water source.

- *Water sources in the home:* hot-water tank, water bed, water in the plumbing, swimming pool, hot tub.

- *Wastewater:* Locate your incoming water valve so you can shut it off if there are reports of disruptions at the local waste-treatment facility. If the outside temperature is below freezing and there is no heat, close and drain your water pipes to prevent them from breaking.

- *If toilets don't function* because a water-supply or waste-disposal facility shuts down temporarily, pour a bucket of wastewater into the toilet to flush.

  - Use rainwater, nondrinkable water from a swimming pool, nearby pond or stream, or dirty ("gray") water previously used for bathing, washing dishes, and so on.

  - If no water source is available, line the toilet with plastic garbage bags, cover waste with lime (available at local gardening stores) or ashes to reduce odors, and dispose daily (bury if possible).

  - Double-bag all waste.

  - If you can, dig a latrine at least fifty feet from the house; cover waste with lime or ashes.

  - Buy a chemical or composting toilet as a neighborhood resource.

My incoming water valve is located:

_____

_____

_____

_____

☐   I have plastic garbage bags and sturdy garbage containers: _____

☐   My wastewater storage containers are:

_____

_____

_____

_____

☐   My waste disposal alternatives are:

_____

_____

_____

_____

☐   I have duct tape and lime or ashes: _____

4. Create as little waste as possible.

    • Paper products reduce water usage but increase waste; burn if possible.

    • Minimize garbage accumulation outside your home. Store in sturdy containers with tight-fitting lids (enough for two weeks of refuse).

5. Develop a neighborhood strategy for emergencies and for people who can't store extra water.

Water Supply, Storage, Purification Resources

Emergency Essentials   800–999–1863

NutriBiotic, Inc.   800–225–4345

Real Goods Renewables   800–919–2400

Walton Feed   800–269–8563

Y2K Solutions Group   888–925–4968

Y2K Supplies   877–580–7844

Making the Best of Basics, by James Talmadge Stevens: available at any large bookstore.

Water is essential to life. Fresh water refreshes our lives. Many countries in the world do not have even the minimum amount of fresh drinkable water people need for basic health and well-being. Setting aside a gallon a day for each member of your family becomes a gesture of love and an expression of gratitude for our abundant way of life.

Chapter 6

THE FOOD SUPPLY

Computers have helped many industries to do away with large inventories. Raw materials or finished products are orchestrated to arrive "just in time" wherever they are needed. Based on this just-in-time philosophy, inventories at grocery stores, drugstores, and most other major retailers are kept to a minimum. Grocery stores and supermarkets in most cities usually carry enough food to feed the local population for only *four or five days*.

At any one moment, computer-controlled refrigerated railroad cars, not grocery stores, contain most of the perishable produce that feeds this nation. While we sleep, next week's dinner is being shipped to the store, just in time. You can imagine the consequences in major population centers if food delivery is interrupted for more than a week for any reason. The shelves will begin to empty, and, at the very least, important food items might not be available.

Railroad and Truck Transport

The railroads deliver fuel for the national power grid and food to every metropolitan area. Every railroad switch in the country depends upon date-sensitive microprocessors that might not function properly after January 1, 2000. This dependence threatens the distribution of electricity from power stations and the delivery of sufficient food to retail outlets. The trucking industry is also managed entirely by computers that tell drivers, via telecommunications, what to transport, where to take it, and when to have it there. A large-scale Y2K computer failure would significantly hamper the nationwide truck fleets.

2
0
0
0

Food

This program recommends that you select foods based on your personal preferences and current eating habits. It offers guidance on the types of food that can be stored safely until the early months of the year 2000. This is not designed to be a long-term food storage program that requires specially packed containers and continual food storage of a year or more. This program encourages you to choose foods from your normal diet that can be readily obtained at your local supermarket. The reserve food supply that you accumulate over the rest of this year is intended to be consumed during the first several months of next year. I encourage you to continue the habit of keeping a reserve food supply for other emergencies. If you want to create a longer-term food-storage program, please refer to the Recommended Resources at the end of this book.

As part of the "Y2K Monthly Program" (chapter 9), you will purchase a one-month supply of eight food categories in separate months. For example:

- The second month is canned-foods month. During that month you accumulate the assortment of canned foods you have chosen for your one-month food reserve.

- The third month is bulk-foods month. During that month you accumulate the assortment of bulk foods you have chosen for your one-month food reserve.

Each month of the "Y2K Monthly Program" contains a detailed list of the specific foods included in each category. Here are some examples:

- canned foods: canned vegetables, fruits, soups, fish, and meat

- bulk foods: oatmeal, rice, corn, flour, beans, ready-to-eat cereals

- dehydrated foods: soups, beans, pasta, ramen, salad dressings, dried fruits

- beverages: canned sodas, boxed juices, bottled water, instant coffee, tea bags

- staples: vegetable oils, spices, sweeteners, sugar, salt, pepper

- vitamins: vitamin C and a daily multivitamin

- snack foods: popcorn, chocolate, cookies, crackers, chips

- high-energy foods: peanut butter, jelly, nutritional bars, trail mix, tofu

Quality

In times of stress and uncertainty, you want to make sure that your family is eating nutrient-dense food that will supply the energy, vitamins, and minerals needed to maintain good health and the ability to cope with adverse conditions. I advise that you purchase foods that have high nutrient content even if such foods may not be the normal ones your family eats. For instance, brown rice provides all the essential B vitamins plus fiber and minerals that white rice, from which nutrient-rich bran is removed, is missing. White rice simply provides starch, which raises the blood sugar but provides little nourishment. After all, what better time to introduce a healthier diet than when your family can't run out to a local fast foods joint to satisfy their junk food cravings!

The following manufacturers of healthy foods are recommended with some of their products mentioned to give you an idea of the range. Try experimenting with these foods during your Y2K practice weekends. You will find these products sold at your local health food store or natural food section at your grocery store. If you can't find them, call the manufacturer for help locating a supplier near you.

- Lundberg Family Farms, P.O. Box 369, Richvale, CA 95974 (530–882–4551)

  - Quick Brown Rice in various flavors such as Spanish Fiesta and Garlic & Basil

  - One Step Entrees in various flavors such as Chili and Curry

  - Risotto in various flavors such as Italian and Creamy Parmesan

- Arrowhead Mills, P.O. Box 2059, Hereford, TX 79045 (800–749–0730)

  - Canned soups in various flavors such as Chicken Vegetable and Mushroom Barley

  - Peanut Butter without hydrogenated oils

  - Instant Oatmeals in various flavors such as Maple & Apple and Cinnamon/Raisin/Almond

- Mercantile Food Co., P.O. Box SS, Philmont, NY 12565 (518–672–0190)

  - American Prairie hot cereals in various flavors such as Creamy Rice & Rye and Maple Raisin & Oats

- Spice Hunter, P.O. Box 8110, San Luis Obispo, CA 93403 (800–444–3061)

  - Quick Pot dinners in various flavors such as Roasted Pepper & Garlic Pasta and Wild Mushroom & Herb Couscous

  - Three-Grain Pasta dishes in various flavors

- Near East, 515 West Main Street, Barrington, IL 60010 (847–842–4654)

  - Rice mixes in various flavors such as Lentil Pilaf and Falafel

  - Couscous in various flavors such as Broccoli and Herb Chicken

  - Pasta with sauces in various flavors such as Tomato Parmesan and Basil & Herb

- Fantastic Foods, 1250 North McDowell Blvd., Petaluma, CA 94954 (707–778–7801)

  - Tofu Burger and Tofu Scrambler dehydrated mixes

  - Instant refried black beans

  - Nature's Burger dehydrated mix

  - Vegetarian Chili dehydrated mix

  - Rice and bean mixes in various flavors such as Curried Basmati Rice with Lentils and Jamaican Black Beans and Brown Rice

- Casbah/Sahara Natural Foods, 14855 Wicks Blvd., San Leandro, CA 94577 (510–352–5111)

  - Mediterranean dehydrated mixes such as Hummus, Falafel, and Baba Ganoush

  - Teapot soups in foil packages for individual servings—15 flavors

  - Couscous and Rice pilafs

  - Perfect Burger dehydrated mix

- Health Valley, P.O. Box 16100 Foothill Blvd., Baldwin Park, CA 91706 (818–334–3241)

  - Canned soups—15 flavors

  - Canned Chili & Beans

- Teeccino, P.O. Box 42259, Santa Barbara, CA 93140 (800–498–3434)

  - Herbal Coffee packed in cans with 3 year shelf life—7 flavors

- Mori-Nu, 2050 West 190th Street, Suite 110, Torrance, CA 90504 (310–787–0200)

  - Tofu in aseptic packages with nine-month shelf life

  - Tofu Mates for making desserts and seasoning tofu dishes in foil packages

Quantity

From your own experience, you must estimate the amount of each type of food your family will need. Here are some guidelines for a family of four:

- canned foods: two to three cans per day for each type of canned food

- bulk foods: grains such as rice or oatmeal, one and a half cups of grain per meal (So if your family eats oatmeal three times per week for breakfast, you will need eighteen cups of oatmeal per month, which weighs approximately four pounds; if your family eats rice three times per week, you'll need about eight pounds because rice is denser than oatmeal)

Storage

Plan on no refrigeration, so purchase prepackaged food (i.e., canned soups, boxed pasta, powdered milk, canned baby formula) that won't spoil until opened. Purchase sizes that can be consumed in one meal so no additional storage is required. Store corn, flour, and beans in plastic containers with tight lids. Label all containers with the contents and date of purchase. Store all food in the coolest, driest, darkest part of your living space. If you live in a cold climate, keep some foods in coolers outside. Protect against animal intrusion.

What Does This Mean for You and Your Family?

- Food might be scarce, and stores may not be supplied for indefinite periods.
- Fresh-food prices might rise dramatically.
- Transportation of goods might be disrupted.
- You might go hungry.

What Can You Do?

- Stock up with a thirty-day supply of canned, bottled, and dried foods.
- Join in a community garden.
- Find local suppliers for critical goods.
- Develop a food-sharing co-op with neighbors.

My Thirty-Day Food Supply

2000

Canned foods:

_____

_____

_____

_____

_____

_____

☐   Bulk foods:

_____

_____

_____

_____

_____

_____

☐   Dehydrated foods:

_____

_____

_____

_____

_____

_____

_____

2000

Beverages:

_____

_____

_____

_____

_____

_____

_____

Staples (oils, spices, sweeteners):

_____

_____

_____

_____

_____

_____

_____

2000

☐   Vitamins:

_____

_____

_____

_____

_____

_____

☐   Snack foods:

_____

_____

_____

_____

_____

_____

2000

High-energy foods:

_____

_____

_____

_____

_____

_____

_____

Pet food:

□

2
0
0
0

_____

_____

_____

_____

_____

_____

_____

We have the luxury in our country of abundant food supplies and safe canning and packaging processes. How fortunate we are! By starting now, you can store enough food for your family, a little bit at a time, without crimping your budget. Don't hoard and don't leave things to the last minute. Your family will be deeply grateful for your planning and foresight. There is no better way to say, "I care."

Chapter 7

HEALTH CARE

When a cardiac monitor stalls, the night nurse isn't aware of the heart attack down the hall.

A machine stamps an incorrect date on a patient's record, leading to a faulty diagnosis and subsequent deadly overdose of medicine.

An extended power outage causes hospital backup generators to fail, and life-support equipment stops.

These are a few of the real concerns facing health-care professionals today. While the possibility of such occurrences is small, the Y2K threat to the health-care community is huge and brings with it substantial risks to patients. About 4 million Americans are treated in a hospital or out-patient setting every day. Rising costs for hospitalization have forced patients with less serious problems into out-patient care, meaning the typical hospital patient today is sicker than he or she was ten years ago. Hospitals are increasingly reliant on electronic monitoring and treatment systems for the seriously ill. The liability associated with medical practice today requires that every hospital carry malpractice insurance in order to keep its doors open. These are the elements that comprise the Y2K threat.

Because of the dependence of health-care on various computerized systems, many medical-care facilities might not operate in the first quarter of next year.

- Some insurance companies might withdraw malpractice insurance for Y2K-related mistakes.

- Power outages and disruptions in communications, food, water, drugs, or medical supplies are likely in some areas.

- Medicare payments might be delayed or not processed at all (because of government noncompliance), forcing hospitals with low profit margins to close.

- Software or embedded-chip failures could cause failures in high-tech medical environments.

We must encourage our health-care providers to be aggressive in addressing the Y2K issue. If you currently depend upon health-care services, I encourage you to investigate the Y2K readiness of your doctor and local hospital. You must also make your own preparations to be self-reliant in case outside services are unavailable.

What Does This Mean for My Family and Me?

- My local hospital might not stay open.

- Equipment in my local hospital might not be reliable.

- Prescription drugs might not be available.

- My medical records may be inaccessible.

What Can I Do?

- Schedule doctor and dental exams before the end of the year.

- Take care of any known medical conditions in 1999.

- Do not schedule surgery or hospitalization during January or February 2000.

- Obtain hard copies of your medical records.

- Have a high-quality first-aid kit in your home. Talk to your local Red Cross chapter about suggested contents.

- Make plans with your health-care provider to have at least a sixty-day supply of any prescription medicines by December 1.

- If you or your family require any life support systems that use electricity, register with your local emergency-management office.

- Have adult family members take a CPR course and elementary first-aid training. Call your local Red Cross chapter for information.

- Check with your local hospital about their Y2K readiness to ensure medical or emergency services will not be interrupted.

Doctor and dental exams I need to schedule before January 1, 2000: ☐

_____

_____

_____

_____

Medical records I wish to obtain: ☐

_____

_____

_____

Components of my first-aid kit should include: ☐

_____

_____

_____

_____

_____

2000

☐   CPR and first-aid plans:

_____

_____

_____

_____

☐   Prescription medications to purchase in advance:

_____

_____

_____

_____

☐   Cold/cough medicines, herbal remedies, and other over-the-counter medications to purchase in advance:

_____

_____

_____

_____

_____

The word health comes from the Old English word for "whole" and "holy." It is truly a holy task to assure the health and happiness of your family. While it might be difficult to imagine health problems before they happen, planning ahead can greatly benefit your family's sense of well-being. Sharing concerns and making plans is an expression of how much you care.

Chapter 8

FAMILY AND COMMUNITY PREPARATION

Your family's sense of security is at the heart of this program. Indeed, the single biggest challenge that national and local leaders face regarding Y2K is how to prevent public fear and panic. John Koskinen, President Clinton's Y2K czar, recently stated that one of his top priorities is to avert "public overreaction" that could prompt a massive run on banks, gas stations, and mutual funds. "Our risk for the country is less likely to be a national infrastructure failure and it's more likely to be a failure either of will or information reporting," he said.

Emotional Preparedness

There are three cornerstones for true Y2K security: (1) household preparedness, (2) emotional preparedness, and (3) community preparedness. The Y2K challenge is not limited only to preparing food, shelter, and warmth to avoid inconvenience. It also includes the opportunity for personal growth and social resilience. I recommend that, along with your household preparations, you explore your potential to prepare yourself, your family, and your community internally—emotionally—for Y2K and other times of stress.

The uncertainty that accompanies Y2K can disrupt our sense of security and cause feelings of increased stress, anxiety, and fear. It is up to each of us to choose how our emotions will affect our family, coworkers, friends, and community. To assist with developing an emotionally balanced response, a Y2K Emotional Preparedness Tool Kit has been designed by the Institute of HeartMath in Boulder Creek, California (800-450-9111, www.heartmath.com).

Based on their ten years of research and training with teachers,

2000

nurses, business executives, police chiefs, and other people, the Institute has assembled a series of emotional self-management tools that can assist people in regaining emotional balance quickly during times of stress and in managing their perceptions and reactions to foster cooperation and commonsense decision-making. A kind of "emotional CPR," the tools are simple and straightforward, and can be rapidly learned. For a thorough background and understanding of the HeartMath program, see the new best-selling book, *The HeartMath Solution* (HarperCollins, 1999).

Family Preparedness

Certain basic supplies and personal necessities, such as toilet paper, personal-care supplies, and kitchen and office supplies, are necessary to keep your family comfortable for several weeks. A suggested list is included in months five and six of the "Y2K Monthly Program." Decide what else you will need, and add it to that month's shopping list.

Air travel at the end of the year will be risky in some parts of the world, and gasoline shortages might limit automobile travel. If you plan to vacation away from home, make plans to stay in that location until the middle of January. Develop alternative means of transportation for work and for shopping. A motor scooter will conserve gasoline. Cross-country skis are a good idea in some parts of the country. Bicycles, skateboards, and roller skates will be helpful in other parts. Develop a daily walking routine by the fall of 1999.

The Y2K problem may affect Internet messages, E-mail, and voice-mail systems. Retrieve any messages by December 30.

The following are steps to check off when dealing with your family's needs during possible Y2K disruptions.

Infants

- Stock up on disposable diapers. Washing clothes may not be possible.

- Have plenty of baby food and snacks handy. Choose items that do not need heating or cooking.

- Buy and set aside four new toys—one for each week of your preparedness month. Choose items that will last a whole week.

- If your baby has any special needs or medications, make prior arrangements with your doctor or drugstore, and stock up on these.

- If baby-sitting is a part of your routine, be sure to plan ahead and make special arrangements with your regular sitters. Remember, phones might not be working, and your sitters will be solving their own problems.

Infant supplies required: ☐

_____

_____

_____

New toys to set aside: ☐

_____

_____

_____

Arrangements with baby-sitters include: ☐

_____

_____

_____

2000

Young Children

The best source of security for young children is a familiar routine and the presence of their parents, so try to maintain reassuring patterns, even in the face of a major disruption—keep the same wake-up time, breakfast, lunch sandwich, nap time, bedtime story, and so on. Try to maintain as much of their ordinary routine as possible.

Preteens

- If schools are closed, set up a home-schooling routine, ideally with other kids and parents. This is where neighborhood planning pays off!

- Buy and set aside four new games that have educational value—one for each week of your preparedness month. Bring them out one week at a time. Make each one a surprise. Choose activities that will challenge the kids at their level, such as word or number games, building sets, or art materials.

- Buy and set aside four new books that they will love. Even if they can read themselves, read at least two of the books aloud together. Remember, there may be no TV for a while.

- Arrange with other families for your kid's best friends to play together, preferably at the same time each day.

- Give your children at least one household task that is appropriate for their age. Include them in the activities of making your home work during Y2K disruptions. It will make them feel valued, useful, and connected.

☐ Other children and parents to participate in home schooling:

_____

_____

_____

_____

_____

Done

Supplies required for my children and teenagers: ☐

_____

_____

_____

_____

Four new games to set aside: ☐

_____

_____

_____

Four new books to set aside: ☐

_____

_____

_____

My children's playmates: ☐

_____

_____

_____

_____

2
0
0
0

☐   Y2K household tasks to assign my children:

_____

_____

_____

_____

Teenagers

- Include teenagers in all planning sessions. Ask for their input and advice. Make them realize you are really counting on them to carry their weight.

- Give your teenagers as many of the household "survival" tasks as possible. Have them help with meals, check supplies, refill oil lamps, chop wood, compost garbage, and so on. This is a time for them to "grow up."

- If school is out, encourage them to volunteer for neighborhood support tasks, such as checking up on the elderly or shut-ins, carrying food to the disabled, helping with transportation. They are much better bike riders and skateboarders than you are! Make them feel valued.

☐   Plans for my family's entertainment needs:

_____

_____

_____

_____

2000

Y2K household tasks to assign to my teenagers: ☐

_____

_____

_____

My teenager's neighborhood support tasks: ☐

_____

_____

_____

_____

_____

The Elderly

- Make sure that the elderly have adequate heat, food, water, and light, especially if they are living alone.

- Assign someone, ideally a young person or close friend, the task of checking up on them regularly.

- Buy and set aside a few new books, games, or hobby project materials that they would enjoy.

- Stock up on special needs, supplies, and medicines that they may require. If they are under professional care, consult with their doctor or nurse ahead of time to be sure they will be cared for.

2000

☐   Arrangements for elderly family members or friends and persons checking on them:

_____

_____

_____

_____

_____

☐   Books, games, or hobby projects to set aside:

_____

_____

_____

_____

☐   Supplies and medicines required by my elderly friends and relatives:

_____

_____

_____

_____

The key for family survival is planning ahead. Y2K can be a special opportunity for you and your family to deepen your bonds and to meet the millennium with a sense of togetherness and adventure.

Developing Community

Community Action and Y2K

Last July I began my exploration of the community role's in Y2K. It started with an evening discussion about Y2K with several friends. Differing points of view came forth during the discussion, from "not a problem" to "get your ammunition and hunker down for the riots." I felt frustrated, angry, and exhilarated through the evening. I was most interested in the idea of "awakening the community to the problem." Later, I reflected on the range of emotions that Y2K inspired.

The next month I went to Boulder, Colorado, to participate with thirty other Y2K activists in a four-day discussion of "What's Next?" For me, this was an in-depth course in Y2K—daily classes melded into informal evening discussions that often stretched far into the night.

The information was alarming. I was scared and angry and inspired and motivated. I recognized that the real challenge of Y2K is that it requires some changes in our relationships—to each other, to the community, to the world. Y2K obliges people and communities to work together to solve a serious common problem.

Today there are community-preparedness groups in several hundred cities across America, and more appear each week. These initiatives have grown out of the belief that if Y2K causes serious disruptions in the societal infrastructure, the best chance for minimizing the impact of such disruptions is to be in a community that is well prepared. Each group has developed its own recommendations for preparedness based upon its unique set of circumstances and beliefs.

In Santa Barbara we have created an expanding Y2K community organization. The first steps to building a community initiative are often the most difficult. Here are the elements that helped our group get started:

1. *Educate yourself.* Meet with others who are aware of the issue and want to spread the word. Exchange views with as many people as you can to really understand how Y2K could impact your community. Recommend that everyone read *The Y2K Citizen's Action Guide,* a short collection of essays on effective citizen responses to the dilemma. Awareness is the first step. (See "Resources.")

2. *Emphasize neighborhood organizing.* The easiest way to expose others to the issue is to talk with your neighbors.

3. *Make contact with local organizations.* Such groups have networks within the community; encourage them to educate others about the issue.

4. *Draw an infrastructure map.* Such a chart of your neighborhood and the broader community could prove helpful in an emergency. Do an inventory of neighborhood resources that could be shared during a Y2K emergency. Identify the neighbors who are unable to care for themselves, and create a plan of assistance for them.

5. *Organize community "off-the-grid" days.* Y2K Neighborhood, a Spokane, Washington, community-preparedness initiative, is promoting a national exercise in "unplugging for a day" every month. They suggest exercises be done in as many communities as possible in 1999 on March 26–27, May 28–29, July 30–31, September 24–25, and November 26–27. The real game begins January 1, 2000!

6. *Assist with programs to support local at-risk populations.* This category includes the homeless, the elderly, the ill and infirm, and the impoverished: all the citizens who are physically or financially unable to provide for themselves during Y2K disruptions.

7. *Work in the spirit of creating a more resilient, more neighborly place to live.* Y2K offers us the opportunity to discover hidden resources within the community that will become significant assets as we move into the twenty-first century.

Preparing our homes and families for possible year-2000 service disruptions is an education in how much our lives rely upon the community around us. These preparations deepen our awareness of how fuzzy are the borders of our homes, neighborhoods, municipalities, states, and countries. Though we might feel more secure as we expand our reserve supply of food and cash, we also recognize that the community around us must be self-sufficient in order for us to realize a true measure of safety within our homes.

Other resources to help me prepare for Y2K: □

_____

_____

_____

_____

_____

Neighbors to discuss Y2K with: □

_____

_____

_____

_____

_____

People in my community who may need Y2K help: □

_____

_____

_____

_____

_____

2000

☐   Local organizations to contact about Y2K:

_____

_____

_____

_____

☐   Community "Off the Grid" days:

_____

_____

_____

_____

_____

2000

This is your opportunity to engage beyond your family and into your community. With your relatives, friends, neighbors, fellow workers, and casual acquaintances, you can build a meaningful web of relations that can hold and support you in any disaster, natural or man-made. The true meaning of community arises from these shared, meaningful efforts. No matter what difficulties might arise with the turning of the century, our collaborations become the glue of true community for the next millennium.

Chapter 9

Y2K MONTHLY PROGRAM

Next Steps

You now have a basic understanding of the Y2K issue and how to prepare yourself for the challenge of the new century. There are many steps in this preparation, but proceeding one step at a time will bring you a sense of personal accomplishment. This monthly preparation program simplifies the task by helping you work regularly for the rest of 1999 toward your preparedness goals. You will gain a feeling of strength and security as you progress through the program.

This chapter has a six-month calendar of activities to begin immediately. I encourage you to do what you can, when you can. You will be surprised at how quickly you begin to feel ready for Y2K. As you proceed, you will develop the confidence that you can make the correct decisions for yourself and your family in the months ahead. Check off the "done" boxes next to the tasks for each month as you complete them, and you'll be on your way!

2000

Done

MONTH 1

Finance and Personal Affairs Month

During this first month you establish a firm foundation of planning for the year ahead. Begin by protecting your assets and making sure you have copies of all important personal records. Watch for news about business and local government preparations.

- ☐ Study this book.
- ☐ Complete the charts on pages 38–42.
- ☐ Make sure you have hard copies of the following documents, and write away for those you don't have:
    - birth certificate
    - Social Security card
    - Personal Earnings and Estimated Benefit Statement
    - educational transcripts/diplomas
    - income tax returns
    - IRS agreements
    - pensions
    - W-2
    - 1099 earning statements
- ☐ Obtain hard copies of these essential documents:
    - real estate deeds and records
    - property tax records
    - proof of all other assets owned
    - mortgages
    - credit card and loan agreements
    - credit report

- insurance policies (add Y2K protection if necessary)

- court judgments

- marriage and divorce records and agreements

- Cash savings: Make the first installment toward your cash reserve for January. ☐

- Ask your banker about your bank's Y2K protection. ☐

- Check the Y2K status of your pension fund and/or 401(K) plan. ☐

- Water storage: Store five gallons of water per month per family member for the next six months to accumulate 30 gallons per person (one gallon per person per day). ☐

2000

MONTH 2

Community Month / Canned Food Month

While continuing preparations at home, begin working with your neighborhood and community. Remember, the better your neighbor is prepared, the better you are prepared.

- [ ] Complete any tasks you identified in the charts on pages 38–42.

- [ ] Pay special attention to home security. Make sure you have enough locks on your windows and doors.

- [ ] If you have an electronic security system, confirm that it is Y2K-compliant.

- [ ] Cash savings: Make the second installment toward your cash reserve for January.

- [ ] "Off-the-grid" practice: Practice living without the service grid for one day. Turn off the electricity or turn off the water for a day.

- [ ] Attend a Y2K meeting in your community.

- [ ] Host a neighborhood meeting. Organize a neighborhood discussion group at your house. Ask someone you know who is familiar with Y2K to assist with the presentation. Discuss how you and your neighbors can share resources and provide common asisstance.

- [ ] Purchase alternative communications equipment.

- [ ] Thirty-day supply of canned foods: Buy foods you like to eat that require the least amount of fuel to prepare.

  - five gallons of water per person

  - two to three cans of food per day for a family of four

  - canned vegetables and fruits

  - canned soups and stews

  - canned fish and meat

  - canned tomato sauces / spaghetti sauce

2000

- canned beans and refried beans
- add your own items

_____

_____

_____

_____

_____

_____

_____

_____

_____

2000

MONTH 3

Local Farm and Garden Month / Bulk Food Month

Visit your local farmer's market. Join a community agricultural cooperative.

☐ • Cash savings: Make the third installment toward your cash reserve for January.

☐ • "Off-the-grid" practice for one day: Go without both water and electricity.

☐ • Begin to pay off all credit-card balances or consolidate them.

☐ • Begin Y2K Christmas shopping. Buy presents for friends and family who need assistance in preparing for next year.

☐ • Join a community cooperative farm program.

☐ • Thirty-day supply of bulk foods: Buy foods you like to eat that require the least amount of fuel to prepare.

Estimate that a family of four eats one and a half cups of grain (rice or oatmeal) at a meal. Determine how many meals per week you would like to eat with grains and multiply by 1.5.

- five gallons of water per person

- oatmeal (quick-cooking oats)

- rice, corn meal, flour, pasta

- other grains—millet, buckwheat, barley, couscous, quinoa

- beans

- ready-to-eat cereals

- nuts (best in the shell)

- bulk–textured vegetable protein (TVP)

- plastic or glass storage containers for the food

- seeds for sprouting during January and sprouting jars

- add your own items

_____

_____

_____

_____

_____

_____

_____

_____

_____

_____

To avoid insect infestation, store all bulk foods in plastic or glass containers with tight-fitting lids. Store in a cool, dark place away from sunlight.

MONTH 4

Health Month / Dehydrated Food Month

Consider your health needs for the winter, and build a reserve of basic supplies. Arrange for your family's health care through the end of the year. Pay attention to any special needs that will require extra care during January.

☐ • Cash savings: Make the fourth installment toward your cash reserve for January.

☐ • "Off-the-grid" practice for two days this month: Don't use your automobile. Walk or ride a bike!

☐ • Schedule medical and dental checkups and/or treatment for completion by early December. Do not schedule hospitalization over the New Year or in January. Obtain copies of all your medical and dental records by early December.

☐ • Schedule CPR and elementary first-aid courses for teenagers and adult family members. Contact local Red Cross or Emergency Services office for information.

☐ • Purchase alternative lighting sources: candles, lanterns, flashlights, batteries.

☐ • Have a Y2K neighborhood party. Have fun with your neighbors while you try out some Y2K ideas. Cook only on the barbecue without electricity. Ask everyone to bring a quart of water and some canned goods for the meal. Listen to music on a battery-operated radio—preferably solar-powered!

☐ • Continue Y2K Christmas shopping.

☐ • Thirty-day supply of dehydrated foods and health supplies: Buy foods you like to eat that require the least amount of fuel to prepare.

   • five gallons of water per person

   • packaged dehydrated bouillon, soups, beans, ramen

   • meal-in-a-cup soups, pastas, polenta, potatoes

2000

- packaged salad dressings, dips, sauces

- dried fruit (store like bulk foods)

- jerky (beef, chicken, fish)

- instant powdered milk

- packaged vegetable burger mixes

- packaged rice pilafs

- vitamins: vitamin C and a daily multivitamin

- high-quality first-aid kit—as recommended by the Red Cross

- over-the-counter medical supplies such as cold medicines and aspirin

- baby needs: diapers, lotion, moist towelettes, disposal bottle liners

- special health needs

- supplies for water and waste treatment including lime and shovel, water filter, water purification tablets, and wastewater storage containers

- add your own items

_____

_____

_____

_____

_____

_____

_____

MONTH 5

Harvest and Fuel Month / Beverages, Snack Foods, and Personal Necessities Month

Prepare your fuel supplies for winter. This month buy your favorite drinks, snack foods, and personal products.

☐ • Cash savings: Make the fifth installment toward your cash reserve for January.

☐ • "Off-the-grid" practice for two days: Go without both water and electricity for both days.

☐ • Winter fuel storage: If you have fuel storage tanks, schedule natural gas or propane deliveries for November or December to insure sufficient reserves.

☐ • Gas stations: Identify all gas stations with hand pumps or backup electrical power near your home.

☐ • Purchase backup cooking equipment: camp stove or barbecue with extra propane bottles and charcoal.

☐ • Purchase equipment for heating living area: wood stove, propane or kerosene heater, fireplace insert.

☐ • Finish Y2K Christmas shopping. Buy an extra lantern, solar-battery charger, water filter, or solar shower.

☐ • Harvest your community/summer garden. Preserve as much food as possible. If you don't have a garden, buy from the local farmer's markets.

☐ • Thirty-day supply of beverages, snack foods, and personal necessities:

  • five gallons of water per person

  • bottled juices and sparkling mineral water

  • packaged juices and canned sodas

  • caffeine-free herbal coffees and herbal teas

  • instant coffee, black or green teas

2000

- powdered beverages, hot chocolate

- snack foods—popcorn, chocolate, cookies, crackers, chips, rice cakes, pretzels

- personal necessities—shampoo, hand soap, shaving cream, razors, hairspray, toothpaste, spare toothbrush, spare eyeglasses, contact lenses and solution, denture needs, and feminine supplies

- add your own items

_____

_____

_____

_____

_____

_____

_____

_____

2000

MONTH 6

Inventory Month / Staples, High-Energy Foods, and Basic Supplies Month

It's time to take a close look at how prepared you are for the year 2000. Do an inventory of your reserve supplies, and write down anything else you will need during the first several months of next year. Consider the difficult times ahead, and buy foods and personal items that give you stability and energy. Make certain you have the necessities that will make life a little easier should the emergency turn out to be more serious than you expected.

☐ • Cash savings: Make the sixth installment toward your cash reserve for January.

☐ • "Off-the-grid practice" for two days: Eat only those types of foods that you have stored in your Y2K supplies.

☐ • Send out letters requesting end-of-year hard copy of important documents: credit reports and creditor detail of your payments toward principal and interest on outstanding debts.

☐ • Thirty-day supply of staples, high-energy foods, and basic supplies:

- • five gallons of water per person

- • staples: vegetable oils, vinegar, sweeteners (honey, sugar, and so on), seasonings (salt, pepper, herbs, spices, tamari)

- • high-energy foods: peanut/almond butter, jelly, nutritional bars, trail mix (store like bulk foods), raisins, tofu

- • paper plates and plastic utensils (don't waste water on washing dishes)

- • nonelectric can opener, Swiss Army knife

- • matches

- • toilet paper, moist towelettes

- • cleaning supplies: liquid detergent, sponges, paper towels, disinfectant

2000

Your Y2K Personal Protection Plan

- plastic bags for good storage; garbage bags for waste disposal

- kitchen supplies: aluminum foil, plastic containers with tight lids

- rubber bands, tape, stapler, staples, scissors

- wrench to shut off gas or water

- other nonelectric tools for construction and repairs

- household bleach

- office supplies: fax paper, envelopes, stationery, pens, Scotch tape

- games, books, nonelectrical entertainment

- add your own items

DECEMBER 1999

Cash and Give Away Month: Enjoy the Holidays

With your current abundance and sense of security, you can give some things away this month. There are people around you who have not been able to prepare adequately. Consider sharing some of your extra supplies with the community. Give some food to a community welfare group. Share your sense of safety with others less fortunate. Fire up the hearth and prepare for a rousing New Year. Plan a wonderful New Year's Eve celebration with your neighbors.

- ☐ Cash savings: Make the last installment toward your cash reserve for January.

- ☐ "Off-the-grid" practice: Take a break this month. You may have plenty of practice next month.

- ☐ Give away some food and supplies. This, then, is the month to share your wealth. There will be people and organizations that are assisting the less fortunate. Give them what you can afford.

- ☐ Finish paying off credit cards. Obtain receipts.

- ☐ Use cash for as many purchases as possible this month. Avoid electronic charges that will span the year date change.

- ☐ Assist your employer with final Y2K preparations.

- ☐ Begin eating perishables/frozen foods during last week of December. If the power goes out, your freezer will stay cold for several days. Minimize the need for keeping food frozen.

- ☐ Some produce will last for several months if stored in a cool, dark place—potatoes, onions, cabbage, and carrots.

- ☐ Fill up the bathtub with water on New Year's Eve. This is a great source of water for washing, flushing the toilet, or other needs if water is unavailable the following week.

- ☐ Enjoy the holidays knowing that you have developed some new skills, are prepared for whatever will occur, and have a new sense of community in your life. Plan a New Year's Eve party and enjoy the date rollover with your Y2K-ready friends and neighbors.

JANUARY 2000

Friends and Family Month

This is the month for which you have been preparing. Take it easy this month. Plan vacation days. Do the things around the house that you normally postpone. Play with the family. Write letters. Appreciate the luxury of slowing down, relaxing during the day, and living self-sufficiently. Meditate on the future. Give thanks for the security that you created for yourself and your family this past year.

- Limit telephone useage on January 1 to 3 to minimize stress on phone infrastructure while any breakdowns are repaired. ☐

- Credit card bills and other bills may not be accurate. Study your receipts of charges that were not billed in 1999, and make certain the billing is accurate. ☐

- Pay cash for all purchases, and get receipts. ☐

- Balance your checkbook, and make sure your January bank statement matches your receipts and records. ☐

- Study your other financial statements for accuracy: investments, mortgage, and other creditors. ☐

- Assist your employer with Y2K recovery activities. ☐

- Offer to assist other people who might not be as prepared as you. ☐

- Pay attention to Y2K news about your community, the nation, and the rest of the world. Consider the long-term impact of global developments on the U.S. situation. ☐

FEBRUARY 2000

Recovery and Readaptation Month

You will now be considering what lies ahead. The state of the nation and the world will have changed somewhat from last year. You need to look into the future, assess your needs and wants, and begin to plan the next phase of your life. This experience has revealed new strengths within you and your family that can be of great benefit in the years ahead. Preserve and cultivate these new talents, interests, and attitudes. Keep your community alive.

- ☐ Credit card bills and other bills might not be accurate. Study your receipts of charges, and make certain the billing is accurate.

- ☐ Balance your checkbook, and make sure your February bank statement matches your receipts and records.

- ☐ Study your other financial statements for accuracy: investments, mortgage, and other creditors.

- ☐ Assist your employer with Y2K recovery activities.

- ☐ Offer to assist other people who might not be as prepared as you.

- ☐ Pay attention to Y2K news about your community, the nation, and the rest of the world. Consider the long-term impact of global developments on the US situation.

Year 2000: The Possibilities Ahead

We have arrived. The new millennium is here, and we have survived—not only survived, but thrived. We have renewed our sense of community and have learned many things about ourselves—what we care about and how we prefer to live. Our family is intact, and our connection to our neighbors and the place we live is deepened. We have reason to be thankful.

We are in charge again. We have looked into the mirror of Y2K and have seen what we need to do to assure a better life for our children and for future generations. There are things we want to do differently. These surely include spending less time working and more time enjoying our blessings.

We know that there is still much to do. Some tasks and needed changes are much clearer now with the experience of Y2K behind us. If the New Year is traditionally a time to make individual resolutions, then a new millennium is a time for us all to make a collective resolution. Let's work together to preserve and deepen the values we care about. Let's reclaim a sense of belonging and of caring not only for our loved ones but for everyone. Let's take care of the natural world that is the basis of all life and every economy.

> As Mahatma Gandhi once suggested, "Almost anything you do will seem insignificant, but it is very important that you do it. . . . We must *be* the change we wish to see in the world."

The joy is in the doing. And we have already begun.

Chapter 10

Y2K CALENDAR

Y2K Flash Dates

The events that happen around these dates will be important barometers of the Y2K situation. Watch for information on television and radio or in newspapers and magazines.

May
Watch for Y2K simulations in business and local governments.

May 28–29

National "off-the-grid" days.

June
Watch for Y2K simulations in business and local governments.

Participate in your communitywide Y2K programs.

Mid-June

Watch for news of federal government Y2K "war games."

New York, Canada, Mexico, and Japan began their fiscal year 2000 on April 1. Noncompliant financial software would cause problems paying bills to state and national service providers. These problems would become evident after two months—during June.

July
Watch for Y2K simulations in business and local governments.

July 1

Forty-six states and Australia begin fiscal year 2000; watch for any problems that will begin to appear over the next three months.

July 6

Nuclear Regulatory Commission determines if nuclear reactors must be shut down for Y2K noncompliance.

July 15

Watch for second-quarter business reports that reveal less progress than anticipated.

July 30–31

National "off-the-grid" days.

August
Watch for Y2K simulations in business and local governments.

August 21–22

Global Positioning Satellite System, used for airplane and ship navigation and location, requires new upgraded hardware to continue functioning accurately after this date. Some users may have navigation problems because of old noncompliant equipment.

September
Watch for Y2K simulations in business and local governments.

September 1

Texas begins its fiscal year 2000; watch for possible difficulties.

September 9

North American Reliability Council conducts second industrywide Y2K test of National Power Control Grid.

2000

September 9

9999 is often used by programmers to tell a computer that a computing task is ended. This day (9/9/99) may confuse computers and cause deletion of data or computer crashes.

September 24–25

National "off-the-grid" days.

October

Watch for Y2K simulations in business and local governments

October 1

U.S. State Department issues country-by-country advisories on Y2K status of foreign countries including assessments of air safety and infrastructure reliability.

Alabama and Michigan begin fiscal year 2000; watch for possible difficulties.

Federal government begins fiscal year 2000; watch for problems.

October 15

Third-quarter business reports are filed.

November

Watch for Y2K simulations in business and local governments.

November 26–27

National "off-the-grid" days.

December

Watch the news.

December 31

Watch the date rollover throughout the day as many parts of the world reach the year 2000 earlier than the United States.

January

Carefully scrutinize all bills for errors.

January 1–8

Watch the Y2K successes and failures; adjust your expectations for the month.

January 15

Assess the state of the country from the news.

February

Carefully scrutinize all bills for errors.

February 29

This is a leap year. Leap years occur every four years, except every one hundred years, when there is no leap year. However, every four hundred years is a leap year. So 1900 was not a leap year and 2000 is a leap year, which could possibly confuse computers.

RECOMMENDED RESOURCES

Books

Awakening: The Upside of Y2K
Edited by Judy Laddon, Tom Atlee, and Larry Shook; available at The Printed Word, 4327 South Perry Street, Spokane, WA 99203 (509–624–3177; 509–747–8776)

Electric Utilities and Y2K
Rick Cowles (self-published, March 1998)

Getting Caught with Your Pantry Down
James T. Stevens (Historical Pubns., 1998)

Making the Best of Basics: Family Preparedness Handbook
James T. Stevens (Gold Leaf Press, 1997)

The Millennium Bug: How to Survive the Coming Chaos
Michael S. Hyatt (Broadway Books, 1999)

The Year 2000 Computer Crisis: An Investor's Survival Guide
Tony Keyes (Y2K Investor, 1997)

The Y2K Personal Survival Guide
Michael S. Hyatt (Regnery Pub., 1999)

Time Bomb 2000
Edward and Jennifer Yourdon (Prentice Hall, 1998); www.yourdon.com

Whatcha Gonna Do If the Grid Goes Down: Preparing Your Household for the Year 2000
Susan Robinson (Virtual Sage, PO Box 100008, Denver, CO 80250)

Y2K Citizen's Action Guide presented by *Utne Reader*
Available: Utne Reader, 1624 Harmon Place, Minneapolis, MI 55403; also available online at www.utne.com/y2k

Y2K: An Action Plan to Protect Yourself, Your Family, Your Assets, and Your Community on January 1, 2000
   Victor Porlier (HarperCollins, 1998)

Year 2000 Personal Protection Guide
   J. R. Morris (Sterlingmoor Pub., Abilene, Tex., 1998); www.y2kpersonal.com

You and the Year 2000: A Practical Guide for Things That Matter
   Jeffrey Shepard, Ph.D. (Indigo Ink, Loveland, Co., 1998)

Catalogs

Real Goods Renewables
Real Goods Trading Company
   www.realgoods.com (800–919–2400)

Y2K Solutions Group
   www.readyfory2k.com (888–y2k–4you)

Y2K Book of Resource Lists: What You Need to Prepare
Practical Preparedness
   www.y2kbookoflists.com (303–665–0650)

Games

Y2K Connections: Building Community, Not Crisis
   www.Y2KConnections.com (800–676–8181)

Videos

Harrabee! Year 2000 Action Pak
   Thorn Tree Productions
   www.russkelly.com/actionpack

Y2K and Us: Facing the Challenge
   National Y2K Civic Leadership Initiative
   E-mail: BDFutures@aol.com (703–525–2251)

Year 2000 Crossroads: A Roadmap for Individual and Family Preparedness
   Cassandra Project and Visual Communications Project
   www.visualcomgroup.com

Year 2000 Home Preparation Guide: Your Home, Your Family, Yourself
   Edward Yourdon, Y2K Solutions Group, Inc. (888–y2k–4you)

INTERNET REFERENCES

Automotive

Automotive Industry Action Group
www.aiagy2k.org (800–279–5187)
For auto industry Y2K inquiries.

Business

Building Owners and Managers Association
www.boma.org/year2000/
Items regarding Y2K for property managers and other property professionals.

Federal Reserve Bank
www.frbsf.org/fiservices/cdc/bulletins.html
The Federal Reserve Bank's site is designed to assist small and medium-sized businesses. The bank wants the materials to be freely distributed.

Small Business Administration
www.sba.gov/y2k/
The Small Business Administration Web site. Includes Y2K checklists for small businesses and links to other checklists.

U.S. House of Representatives Small Business Committee
www.house.gov/smbiz/leg/y2k.html
The site has checklists, Committee hearing testimony, listings of research papers, helpful links, and press releases.

Y2K Guide for Small to Midsize Businesses
www.y2kexperts.com/certified_y2k_ready/index.htm
Y2K information for small and midsize businesses.

Christian-Based Y2K Efforts

Larry Burkett

www.cfcministry.org

Larry Burkett's Christian Financial Concepts Y2K position paper and other valuable Y2K information.

Christian Y2K: Year 2000

www.christiany2k.com

To provide evangelical Christians with balanced information from a variety of sources and perspectives, so that people of faith can be informed about the issue of Y2K.

Christian Broadcasting Network

www.cbn.org/y2k

Christian Broadcasting Network' s Y2K resource center gives you a broad overview and insights into Y2K.

Project Joseph

www.josephproject2000.org

Dedicated to preparing the Church to serve during Y2K by working with local Christian leadership in readying homes, churches, businesses, and communities.

Y2K Prayer Shield

www.y2kprayershield.org

Their vision is to function as an intercessory network for Y2K efforts with a special focus on the advancements of Project Joseph.

Community Efforts

Arlington Institute (John Petersen)

www.arlingtoninstitute.org (703–812–7900)

This institute develops future scenarios and contingency plans to adapt to possible social changes. With the Global Action Plan, the institute is establishing a national community preparedness campaign. In collaboration with Y2K Today, the institute is developing a Web-based global network connecting up to 40,000 local community preparedness groups. Web site offers an extensive range of reliable information, news, and resources.

Berkana Institute (Meg Wheatley)

www.angelfire.com/ca/rhomer/social.html

Specializes in the future of social organization. Wheatley and Myron Kellner-Rogers have written extensively on Y2K.

Boulder Year 2000 Community Preparedness Group (Margo King)

www.y2kboulder.com

While their immediate concern is the City of Boulder, much of the material should be useful to every community addressing the various Y2K concerns.

Carmichael, Doug

www.tmn.com/y2k

For an exploration of the social causes and impacts of Y2K, and as a place for reflective thinking, see social psychologist Doug Carmichael's site.

Cassandra Project

www.millennia-bcs.com

www.cassandraproject.org/home.html

National clearinghouse for personal and community Y2K preparedness effort. Also has Spanish translated publications.

Center for Visionary Leadership

www.visionarylead.org

Psychological and spiritual dimensions of Y2K and community preparedness.

Citizens for Y2K Recovery

www.cy2kr.com

This is a grassroots, educational, multiservice membership organization dedicated to helping individual communities prepare for and recover from the disruptions of Y2K. They are forming local chapters across the country.

Coalition 2000

www.coalition2000.org (410–730–5677)

A clearinghouse of credible Y2K information for community, government, and private sector groups. Working with the President's Council on Year 2000 Conversion, Coalition 2000 develops and distributes Y2K best practices manuals to educate people about Y2K preparedness.

Co-Intelligence Institute (Tom Atlee)

www.co-intelligence.org/Y2K.html

With a focus on Y2K as an opportunity to transform our relationships to one another and to the earth.

Davis Logic LLC (Steve Davis)

www.erols.com/steve451/

Y2K coordination among businesses, local government, and community.

Global Millennium Foundation

www.globalmf.org

Comprehensive information about Y2K and Canada.

New Heaven New Earth (NHNE)

www.nhne.com

Involved in community preparedness for Y2K, specifically with connections to Sedona, Ariz., and their Action Group. See their Y2K Web site: www.wild2k.com

NOVA–Y2K

www.novay2k.org

Information on Y2K community organization.

Resilient Communities Project (Robert Theobald)

www.resilientcommunities.org

www.transform.org

Robert Theobald has been working on fundamental change issues for four decades. The multiplying forces of Y2K, global warming, and worldwide economic crisis create a unique context and opportunity to spread the need for fundamental change.

Y2K Community Project

www.y2kcommunity.org

This is an active virtual community that offers support to local communities to help them become healthy and vibrant, focusing on community resilience worldwide and Y2K preparedness.

Y2K Connections: Building Community, Not Crisis

www.PrepareForY2K.com/game.html (800–676–8181)

Y2K Connections is a community-building game. It presents players with potential real-life Y2K situations and seeks to creatively solve the problems through collaboration.

Y2K Neighborhood (Judy Laddon)

509–624–3177

Articles on neighborhood preparedness and positive visions of the future.

Computers

Apple Computer

www.apple.com/about/year2000/index.html
Apple Computers' Year 2000 site.

Cory Hamasaki's Current DC Y2K Weather Reports

www.kiyoinc.com/current.html
Find out what professional programmers are doing and thinking about current Y2K news and developments.

Computer Manufacturers

www.compinfo.co.uk/y2k/manufpos.htm
Links to computer manufacturers' home pages with Y2K information.

IBM

www.ibm.com/IBM/year2000
IBM's Year 2000 site.

Microsoft Computer

www.microsoft.com/year2000
Microsoft's Year 2000 site.

PC Magazine

www.8.zdnet.com/pcmag/special/y2k/index.html
PC Magazine and ZDNet host PC Magazine Year 2000 Resource Center.

QuickFix 2000

877–806–4383
Effective software package that will fix most Y2K personal computer problems.

TEST 2000

www.rightime.com
Download free Y2K testing software for PCs.

Consumer Products

Consumer Electronics Manufacturers Association (CEMA)

www.cemacity.org/cemacity/govt/cema2000.htm
This is a good site to obtain numbers and sites for suppliers.

EDS Corporation

www.eds.com/vendor2000

Lists Y2K-compliance status of 125,000+ specific products by brand, model, and serial numbers.

Federal Trade Commission
www.ftc.gov (202–382–4357)
Y2K survey of consumer electronic products and manufacturer Web sites.

Information Technology Association of America (ITAA)
www.itaa.org/year2000.htm
Nonprofit professional computer society tracking Y2K. Site includes links to vendors that provide Y2K products and services.

Vendors
www.vendor2000.com
A searchable database of vendors and their products. Usually a link to manufacturer's Web site is included.

Economy and Finance

Grabow, Dennis (Millennium Investment Corp.)
www.millenniuminvest.com (312–595–6526)
Leading authority on the global financial implications and the investment opportunities surrounding Y2K. Millennium Investment Corp. is a private investment management firm that focuses on the immediate and long-term investment aspects of Y2K.

Keyes, Tony
www.y2kinvestor.com/intro.html (703–893–8808 for monthly newsletter)
This Web site examines the financial side of Y2K problems—good links, informative discussion board.

Tantleff, Michael (Prudential Securities)
800–368–9370
Senior Vice President for Investments, Prudential Securities, Santa Barbara. Very successful investment broker who has a special expertise in Y2K. I highly recommend him for his skills in understanding market trends and his ability to successfully manage portfolios during both growth and recessed economic times.

Yardeni, Dr. Ed
www.yardeni.com/cyber.html
A comprehensive overview of all sectors of the economy from government

agencies to banking, insurance, and all infrastructure. Includes updates on current status of remediation efforts in all sectors.

Yardeni, Dr. Ed, Y2K News Fax Service

www.yardeni.com/y2knews.html (212–469–5717)

Resource for those wanting to send or receive a hard copy of recent Y2K news stories that are clipped from newspapers around the world.

Government

Davis Logic LLC (Steve Davis)

www.erols.com/steve451/

Y2K coordination among businesses, local government, and community.

Federal Government

www.itpolicy.gsa.gov/mks/yr2000/y2khome.htm

U.S. Federal Government gateway for Year 2000 Information Directories. Also has links for children to write in with comments or questions.

Federal Y2K Information Center

888–USA–4Y2K; 888–872–4925

Provides a "one-stop" source to disseminate Y2K information, answers to Y2K-related questions, manufacturer information referrals, and pro and con information regarding Y2K "rumors" to the public.

FEMA (Federal Emergency Management Agency)

www.fema.gov

The federal organization that oversees recovery from emergencies offers guidelines for Y2K risks and preparation.

GAO (General Accounting Office)

www.gao.gov/y2kr.htm

GAO's information on government readiness. Documents can be ordered online or by calling 202–512–6000.

Municipal Government Checklist

www.angelfire.com/mn/inforest/capersj989.html

For local government.

National Association of State Information Resource Executives

www.nasire.org/ss/ST2000.html

The association for state information-technology officers. Information on states that have Y2K Web sites.

National Institute of Science and Technology

www.nist.gov/y2k/

This agency of the U.S. Dept. of Commerce's Technology Administration maintains a site that contains free software, Y2K assistance for small manufacturers, and links to other informative sites.

President's Council on Year 2000 Conversion

www.y2k.gov

This site provides information on official Y2K policy and actions including links to other useful Year 2000 Web sites.

Also, write with comments or questions to:

Year 2000 Team (MKS)
U.S. General Services Administration
Office of Governmentwide Policy
1800 F St. NW, Room 2014
Washington, DC 20405

Public Technology, Inc.

www.pti.org/membership/y2k

For local government.

Senate Special Committee on the Year 2000 Technology Problem

www.senate.gov/~y2k

Up-to-date reports of ongoing Senate hearings and research findings on Y2K.

Social Security Administration

www.ssa.gov

Year 2000 information for the Social Security Administration and forms to request Personal Earnings and Estimated Benefit Statement.

Subcommittee on Government Management, Information and Technology

www.house.gov/reform/gmit/y2k/index.htm

U.S. government Y2K compliancy grades.

Summary of Oversight Findings and Recommendations

www.house.gov/reform/gmit/y2k/y2k_report/Isummary.htm

Senator Paul Horn rates government offices on Y2K.

Washington DC Year 2000 Group

www.monumental.com/bwebster/y2k

www.csis.org/html/y2kpress.html#3

This group has a membership of over 1,000 from government, military, cor-porations, education, law, contractors, consultants, and vendors.

What is your state doing about Y2K?
www.y2k.gov/java/abouty2k6.html

Y2K Preparedness City Action Councils
www.Y2knet.com (877–4–Y2KCPR)
To educate civic leaders about Y2K—providing free literature, audio, and video.

Y2K Tri-State Planning Group—New York Metropolitan Region
www.y2k3states.org
Collaborative effort to enable various organizations to share their knowledge and experience in dealing with potential Y2K problems that could affect their region.

Health Care

American Red Cross
www.redcross.org/disaster/safety/y2k.html
Y2K-preparedness recommendations to safeguard health.

Food and Drug Administration
www.fda.gov
Year 2000 impact on biomedical equipment and other Year 2000 sites. General info.

Public Health Information
www.cdc.gov/year2000.htm
Implications for Public Health Information and Surveillance systems from the Centers for Disease Control and Prevention.

RX 2000 Solutions Institute (Joel Ackerman)
www.rx2000.org
Best overview of the healthcare industry. Downloadable checklists and infor-mation for health-oriented organizations.

Year 2000 Consulting (Laurene West)
E-mail: llw@integrityonline3.com
Specialist in healthcare compliance and the medically dependent.

Infrastructure

Electric Utilities and Year 2000 (Rick Cowles)

www.euy2k.com

Rick is considered the nation's foremost expert on the subject of Y2K and electric power grids.

Frautschi, Dr. Mark

www.tmn.com/~frautsch/y2k2.html

An excellent and thorough research paper on embedded systems can be found at his Web site.

North American Electric Reliability Council

www.nerc.com

Coordinating agency for regional power networks of North America.

Nuclear Regulatory Commission

www.nrc.gov/NRC/NEWS/year2000.html

Information on Y2K status of nuclear power plants.

Utilities and Year 2000

www.accsyst.com/writers/ele2000a.htm

Information about Y2K and the utilities industry.

Year 2000 Paul Revere Community Alert (Roleigh Martin)

ourworld.compuserve.com/homepages/roleigh_martin

Roleigh Martin is a specialist on embedded systems and the infrastructure. He provides excellent general information on Y2K and valuable links to other sites.

Legal

General

www.y2k.com/index.htm

Y2K legal information and links to other related sites.

General References (Timothy J. Feathers)

www.year2000.com/archive/warranty.html

Y2K-compliance warranty language.

General References (Williams, Mullen, Christian & Dobbins)

www.y2k.com/negotiat.htm

Negotiating Y2K remediation contracts.

Pre-Paid Legal Services

800–431–8974

Provides legal advice and counsel on personal and business affairs for low monthly fee.

News

deJaeger, Peter (The Year 2000 Information Center)

www.year2000.com

Broad view of Y2K issues with a variety of news articles, information on legal and technical aspects, vendors, and daily world updates.

IT2000

www.it2000.com

National bulletin board for Year 2000.

Millennium Salons

home.ica.net/~njarc/msalons/main.html

Using a discussion forum and database of important information, this Web site is creating a library of practical information concerning what to do about the Y2K problem.

New Heaven New Earth (NHNE)

www.nhne.com

Provides excellent weekly summary of news stories, facts, and important issues about Y2K.

Gary North's Y2K Links and Forum

www.garynorth.com/y2k/index.cfm

www.garynorth.com/y2k/search_.cfm

One of the earliest alerts on Y2K-related issues. Maintaining an extensive Y2K database, North updates his site daily with news stories and commentary.

The Registry

www.year2000registry.com (416–675–1515)

This is the central registry that coordinates the communication of up-to-date Year 2000 Readiness Statements and Advisories—for all organizations, products, services, governments, and industries, worldwide.

Sanger's Review of the Millennium

www.cruxnet.com/~sanger/y2k/

This is a daily summary of the news about Y2K.

Alan Simpson's Comlinks

www.comlinks.com

One of the leading commentators on Y2K. Valuable information and frequent updates.

Westergaard Year 2000

www.y2ktimebomb.com

Provides readers with up-to-date news and critical analysis of economic, political, and social issues surrounding Y2K. Also provides E-mail summaries of top Y2K stories.

Yourdon, Edward

www.yourdon.com/index.htm

Edward Yourdon is the author of Time Bomb 2000 and a leading Y2K commentator and analyst.

Y2K Today

www.y2ktoday.com

The most significant website for Y2K news that reports daily on national and global events. Y2K Today is developing, with the Arlington Institute, a Web-based global network connecting up to 40,000 local community preparedness groups.

Y2K Links

www.y2klinks.com

This group of Web sites dedicated to Y2K combines the largest Y2K resource on the Net.

Y2K News

www.y2knews.com (Fax: 931–484–8825)

Y2K publishes a biweekly, hardcopy magazine that is an excellent resource. Now offering bulk quantities for churches, schools, and community groups.

Nonprofit

Adopt-a-Charity

www.asimpson.com/adopt/chmenu.htm

An on-line exchange for Y2K or computer professionals and nonprofit organizations.

Nathan Cummins Foundation

www.ncf.org

Y2K foundations and philanthropy.

Gifts in Kind International

www.GiftsInKind.org/y2k.htm

This site includes action plans, checklists, and sample letters.

United Way

www.unitedway.org/year2000

This guide has been developed to help your United Way develop a Y2K plan to assess if you have risks and how you may choose to address them.

Personal Preparedness

American Red Cross's Safety Y2K: What You Can Do to Be Prepared

www.redcross.org/disaster/safety/y2k.html

Web site for Red Cross and personal preparedness.

Ark Institute

www.arkinstitute.com

Focuses on personal preparedness supplies. Excellent resource on seed information.

Carmichael, Doug

www.tmn.com/y2k

For an exploration of the social causes and impacts of Y2K, and as a place for reflective thinking, see social psychologist Doug Carmichael's site.

Citizens for Y2K Recovery Newsletter

www.CY2KR.com/Mailinglist.html

Newsletter (electronic or printed form) focuses on the "nuts and bolts" of preparing for Y2K, and also includes timely developments in the news.

Federal Y2K Information Center

888–USA–4Y2K; 888–872–4925

Provides a "one-stop" source to disseminate Y2K information, answers to Y2K-related questions, manufacturer information referrals, and pro and con information regarding Y2K "rumors" to the public.

Food Storage FAQ

www.survival-center.com/foodfaq/ff1-toc.htm

Questions and answers about survival issues.

Hickman, James

www.wayfinder.com/year2000

The author of this book, and a specialist on Y2K education and preparedness. Web site provides information on other materials available.

Hyatt, Michael

www.y2kprep.com (888–Y2K–PREP)
Focus is on understanding the problem and steps for preparation.

Lord, Jim

www.survivey2k.com
Personal preparedness. One of most popular educators on Y2K issues.

Mazel's Nutritional Foods

www.dheaconnection.com/nitro/index.hi
Offers bulk food paks from Mountain Hous Alpine Aire and NitroPak.

Noah's Ark: Emergency Preparedness Information

www.millenium-ark.net/News_Files/Hollys.html
Information on emergency preparedness.

PermaPak Emergency Food Supplies

877–600–3663
Source for dehydrated food and other emergency survival supplies.

Personal Y2K Supplies

www.y2klinks.net/y2ksupplies.html
A comprehensive list of all supplies needed for Y2K.

Preparing for the Year 2000 Crash (Scott Olmsted)

www.prepare4y2k.com
Individual preparedness site by a well-known computer programmer who recognized the Y2K problem early and has developed preparedness guidelines.

Project Noah: Family Preparedness

www.chasedata.com/storage

Rogue Valley Y2K Task Force

www.rv-y2k.org/prepindv.htm
Individual and household preparedness.

Walton Feed

www.waltonfeed.com/self/default.htm (800–847–0465)
Certified organic foods and 72-hour kits.

Wiley, Julianne

www.justpeace.org/nuggetsindex.htm
Exhaustive data on personal preparedness

Y2K Chaos: The Survival Site

www.y2kchaos.com
Personal preparedness.

Y2K for Women

www.y2kwomen.com
Designed to explain the Year 2000 problem and provide encouragement to women concerning Y2K issues.

Y2K Solutions Group, Inc.

www.readyfory2k.com (888–Y2K–4YOU)
The Y2K Solutions Group—Edward and Jennifer Yourdon, James Talmage Stevens—provides sources for personal survival items, books and videos, food storage, water storage, etc.

INDEX

Personal computer, 46–48
   upgrading, 47–48
Personal preparedness, Internet
   resources for, 122–24
Police emergencies, 2
Power generating plants, 6
Power shortages or failure, 7–8, 37, 71
Power surges, 46
Pre-Paid Legal Services, 33–34
Prescription medications, 72, 74
Propane gas heaters, 11
Property deeds, 32
Property tax records, 32

Quicken, 48
Quick Fix 2000, 47

Radio, 2
   using alternative power sources, 4
Railroads, 7, 60
Real estate records, 32
Real Goods Renewables, 8, 10, 59
Red Cross, 73
Resources, 108–10
   see also Internet references
   books, 108–9
   catalogs, 109
   games, 109
   videos, 109
Rice, 62
RJK Power, 8

Satellites, 1–2, 105
Sears, 8
Security systems, 35, 45
Shortwave radio, 4
Simulations, of Y2K, 104
Smoke alarms, 11
Social Security card, 32
Solar panels, 10
Spice Hunter, 63
Spreadsheets, 48
Sprinkler systems, 35
Stocks, 28
Surge protectors, 46

Teeccino, 64
Teenagers, 80–81
Telephones, 1, 2, 3, 35
Televisions, 1–2
   battery-powered, 4
1099 earning statements, 32

Toilets, 57
Toyota, 46
Transportation
   alternative means of, 13–14, 76
   carpools, 13, 15
   gasoline, 7, 8
   Internet resources, 110
   microprocessors, 46
   railroads, 7, 60
   travel/vacations, 76
   trucks, 60
TransUnion, 29
Travel, 76
Traveler's Friend, 56
Truck transport, of food, 60

U.S. State Department advisories, 106
Uniden CB radios, 3
Utilities, 35
   alternatives to local, 8
   electricity, 6–7

Vacations, 76
VCRs, 45
Vendors, 52
VitalChek, 32
Vogelzang International Corp., 11
Voicemail systems, 76
Volcano Corporation, 8
Voter registration records, 32

W–2 forms, 32
Walkie-talkies, 3
Wal-Mart, 8, 11
Walton Feed, 54, 59
War games, 104
Waste treatment, 53
Water
   daily use/storage/sources, 54–56
   heating of, 7, 45
   resources, 58–59
   supplies and treatment, 53–59
Wood stoves, 10–11

Y2K calendar, 104–7
Y2K Citizen's Action Guide, 83
Y2K Emotional Preparedness Tool Kit,
   75
Y2K monthly program. *See* Monthly
   program
Y2K Solutions Group, 8, 10, 11, 59
Y2K Supplies, 59